The ELEMENTS

The
ELEM

ENTS

DAN GREEN

SCHOLASTIC discover more™

How to discover more

This book is simple to use and enjoy, but knowing a little bit about how it works will help you discover more about the elements. Have a great read!

How the pages work

The book is divided into chapters, such as **Nonmetals and gases**. Each chapter is made up of stand-alone spreads (double pages) that focus on specific topics.

History of discovery
From cave paintings to diamonds in space, the last section of this book (pages 98–105) tracks elemental discoveries through the centuries.

Element info
Colored boxes give the atomic number of an element, its symbol, and its name.

Introduction
Most spreads have a general introduction to the subject.

Fantastic facts
BIG text gives an amazing fact or quote!

Spread heading
The title of the spread lets you know what the subject is.

Fact boxes
Some spreads include a profile box with details about a specific element.

Oxygen [The spark of life]

8
O
OXYGEN

As a component of water, oxygen covers most of the planet's surface and is vital for life. And as a gas that makes up 21 percent of the air that you breathe, oxygen drives chemical processes in your body. This reactive element is also at the heart of every fire that burns.

Oxygen (O₂)
An oxygen gas molecule is made up of two linked oxygen atoms.

Element profile

Name	Oxygen
Symbol	O
Atomic number	8
What it is	A colorless, odorless gas
Melting point	-360.9°F (-218.3°C)
Boiling point	-297.2°F (-182.9°C)
Special features	Most common element in Earth's crust; essential for life; light blue as a liquid

The great reactor
Oxygen is very reactive. Burning, for example, is a reaction between a substance, such as wood, and oxygen in the air. Because of oxygen's reactivity, most of Earth's oxygen is locked up in the crust, bound to other elements as oxide compounds.

Ancient air
The atmosphere of the young Earth would have been deadly to us, since it contained no oxygen. Gradually, oxygen began to build up in the air as it was released by ocean life-forms called blue-green algae.

Giant dragonfly fossil
Around 300 million years ago, atmospheric oxygen reached a peak of 35 percent, allowing insects, such as Meganeura, to grow to giant sizes.

Meganeura's wingspan was over 2.5 feet (75 cm).

Oxygen in the atmosphere began building up 2.5 billion years ago

Wrapped in gas
Earth's atmosphere is mostly oxygen and nitrogen, with small amounts of other gases. There are layers within the atmosphere, with a different temperature and a slightly different mix of gases. The ozone layer is rich in a form of oxygen called ozone.

Ozone (O₃)
An ozone molecule consists of three oxygen atoms. The ozone layer protects living things from the Sun's harmful ultraviolet (UV) rays.

The oxygen makers
Plankton are tiny ocean-living plants, animals, and microbes, such as this blue-green alga. Plankton create about 70 percent of the oxygen in the air by photosynthesis (see page 90).

Digital companion book

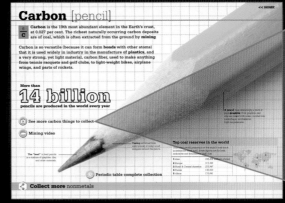

Carbon [pencil]

C

Carbon is the 19th most abundant element in the Earth's crust, at 0.027 per cent. The richest naturally occurring carbon deposits are of coal, which is often extracted from the ground by **mining**.

Carbon is so versatile (because it can form **bonds** with other atoms) that it is used widely in industry in the manufacture of **plastics**, and a very strong, yet light material, carbon fiber, used to make anything from tennis racquets and golf clubs, to light-weight bikes, airplane wings, and parts of rockets.

More than 14 billion
pencils are produced in the world every year

See more carbon things to collect

Mining video

Collect more nonmetals

Collect every element from the periodic table.

Nonmetals [the popu...

Carbon, along with nitrogen, oxygen, phosp... selenium are nonmetals. You'll find them in... of things. Nitrogen is used to freeze foods, i... even in the ball bearings of many skateboa... to preserve food, bleach textiles, and create... phosphorus is used in fertilizers and deterg... a mineral in some foods, is also used in dan...

Periodic table complete collection

Nitrogen

Sulfur

Click for great ideas ...
your collection.

More here columns
This feature suggests books to read, places to visit, experiments to do, and keywords to learn.

Spread types

Look out for different kinds of spreads such as catalog spreads and feature spreads. There are others, too—that's what makes the book so interesting.

82/83
NONMETALS & GASES

More here

ozone layer forest fire cyanobacteria **plankton** **stromatolite** respiration combustion **death zone** **water** liquid oxygen atmosphere **ultraviolet** **distillation** *Meganeura*

Get experimenting!
To see how burning relies on oxygen, ask an adult to place an upturned glass jar over a lighted candle. The flame will go out, but only after it has used up all the oxygen in the jar.

burning: a chemical reaction in which a substance combines with oxygen, releasing heat.

distillation: the process of heating a liquid mixture to separate out its components. To distill air, the air has to first be cooled so that it turns into a liquid.

photosynthesis: the process by which plants use the energy in sunlight to make food from carbon dioxide and water. Oxygen is released as a waste product (see pages 90–91).

Making oxygen
The oxygen needed for industrial processes such as steelmaking (see page 58) is obtained from air by a process known as distillation. This "manufactured" oxygen is also used in hospitals and aircraft.

Lifesaving gas
Manufactured oxygen allows astronauts, mountain climbers, and divers to breathe in extreme and dangerous environments.

THERMOSPHERE
53–430 miles (85–690 km)

MESOSPHERE
31–53 miles (50–85 km)

STRATOSPHERE
12–31 miles (20–50 km)

OZONE LAYER

TROPOSPHERE
0–12 miles (0–20 km)

OSPHERE   EARTH

Key to symbols in More here columns

Suggested reading

Keywords for web searches

Fact file

Experiment

Mini-glossary

Places to visit

View from afar

Mini-glossary
This explains challenging words and phrases found on the spread.

Identity labels
Many pictures have labels to tell you exactly what they are.

Alkaline earth metals [The upper-crust elements] 36/37

CATALOG SPREAD

A catalog spread is packed full of information about a particular group of elements and their uses.

Copper [Old faithful] 54/55

HISTORY SPREAD

A timeline column gives you the most important dates and events in the history of a topic.

PHOTOGRAPHIC SPREAD

This type of spread focuses on an extraordinary subject, often providing an unfamiliar view, such as this worker wearing fireproof clothing in a blast furnace.

Glossary and index

The glossary explains words and phrases that might not be explained fully on the spread or in the **More here** column. The index can help you find pages throughout the book on which words and topics appear.

Mining [digging deep]

Fast, modern conveyor belts shift
16,000 lbs
of coal a minute from the mines

Read in-depth element encyclopedia entries.

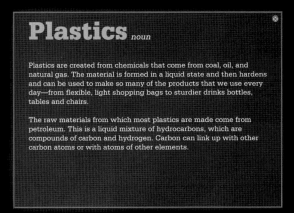

Plastics *noun*

Plastics are created from chemicals that come from coal, oil, and natural gas. The material is formed in a liquid state and then hardens and can be used to make so many of the products that we use every day—from flexible, light shopping bags to sturdier drinks bottles, tables and chairs.

The raw materials from which most plastics are made come from petroleum. This is a liquid mixture of hydrocarbons, which are compounds of carbon and hydrogen. Carbon can link up with other carbon atoms or with atoms of other elements.

Look up element words.

Consultant: Dr. Paul Lickiss, Department of Chemistry, Imperial College, London

Literacy consultant: Jane E. Mekkelsen, Literacy & Learning Connections LLC

Project editors: Steve Setford, Susan Malyan

Project art editor: Mark Lloyd

Designer: Clare Joyce

US editors: Elizabeth Hester, Beth Sutinis

Art director: Bryn Walls

Managing editor: Miranda Smith

Cover designer: Natalie Godwin

DTP: John Goldsmid

Visual content editors: Alan Gottlieb, Dwayne Howard

Executive Director of Photography, Scholastic: Steve Diamond

"We must expect the discovery of many as yet unknown elements."

—DMITRI MENDELEEV

Library of Congress Cataloging-in-Publication Data Available

ISBN 978-0-545-33019-0

10 9 8 7 6 5 4 3 2 1   12 13 14 15 16

Printed in Singapore   46
First edition, January 2012

Scholastic is constantly working to lessen the environmental impact of our manufacturing processes. To view our industry-leading paper procurement policy, visit www.scholastic.com/paperpolicy.

Contents

Meet the elements

What is an element?	14
Everyday elements	16
Atoms	18
Making elements	20
The periodic table	22
Gallery	24

Fiery & fizzing metals

Fiery & fizzing metals	28
Alkali metals	30
Hydrogen	32
Alkaline earth metals	36
Calcium	38

Mainstream metals

Mainstream metals	44
Earth	46
Transition metals	48
Gold	52
Copper	54
Elements in art	56
Iron	58
Rare earth metals	62
Heavy elements	63
Radioactive elements	64
Poor metals	68
Metalloids	72

Nonmetals & gases

Nonmetals & gases	76
Deadly elements	78
Nonmetals	80
Oxygen	82
Human body	84
Carbon	88
Carbon for life	90
Halogens	92
Noble gases	94

History of discovery

Element quest	100
New ideas	102
Creating elements	104
Glossary	106
Index	109
Credits and acknowledgments	112

Crystal cave

Elements make up our world, and they can create awesome natural structures. Here, calcium (see pages 38–39), oxygen (see pages 82–83), and sulfur (see page 80) have combined to form vast crystals of selenite. The giant pillars—the world's largest known crystals—are up to 33 feet (10 m) long and 55 tons in weight. They formed over 500,000 years from mineral-rich hot water that circulated through caverns in Chihuahua, Mexico.

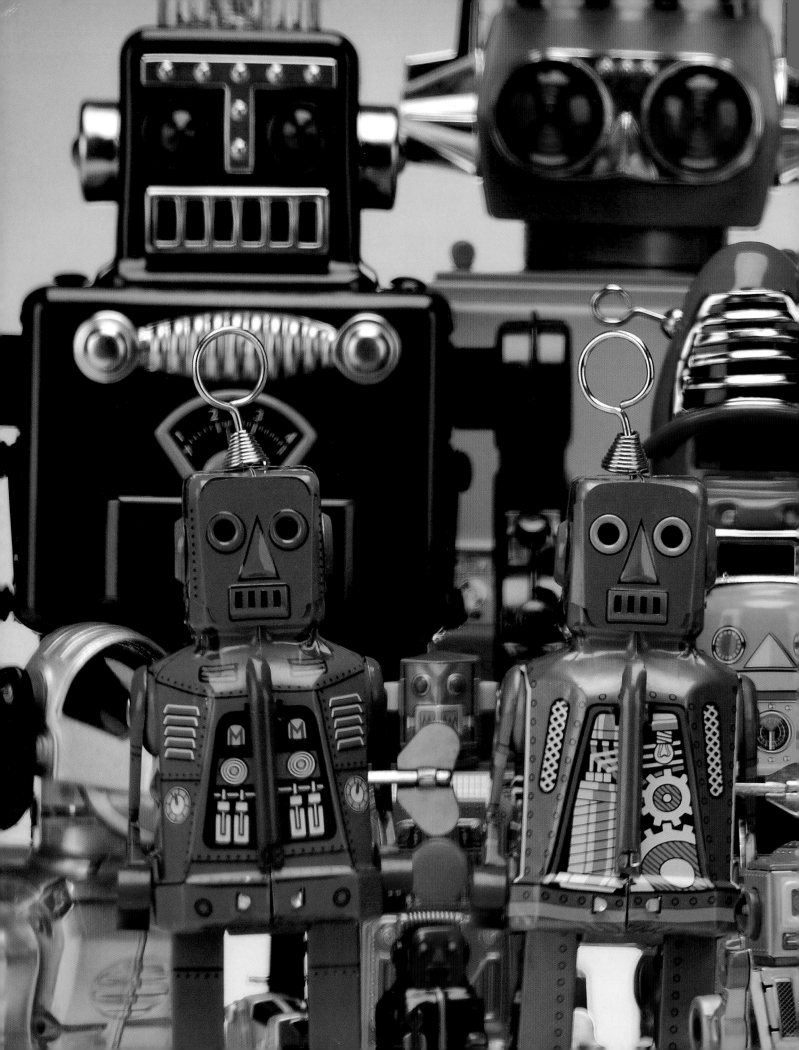

Robots on parade

One of the great things about elements is that we can combine and process them to make all sorts of fun stuff, such as these toy robots. Elements can be metals or nonmetals. Most metals can be bent and shaped into any form you like, and many are superdurable, too. The bodies of these space-age robots are made from steel (see page 58) that has been given a thin coating of tin (see page 68). They are pressed into shape in molds.

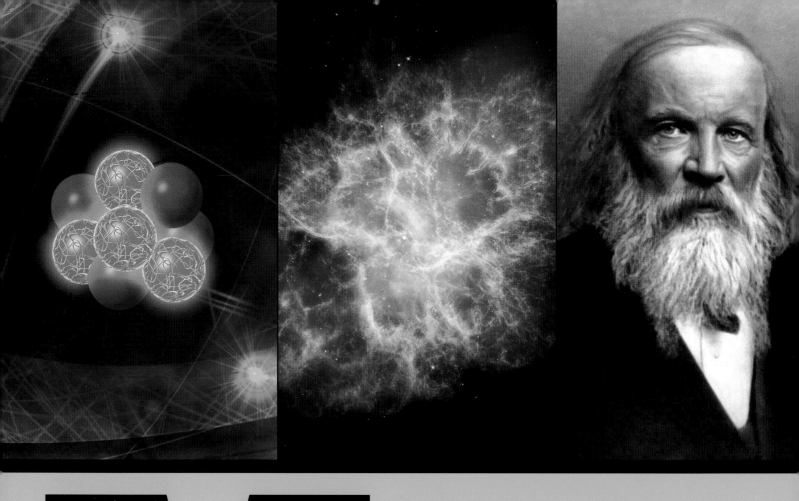

Mee
elem

* What's inside a beryllium atom?

* Where do elements come from?

* Who devised the periodic table of elements?

the

ents

What is an element? [The

The stuff that's all around us is matter—from specks of dust and this book to phones, skyscrapers, and the Sun. Matter is made up of a mind-boggling number of combinations of 114 basic substances called elements. Only 92 elements occur naturally. The rest are synthetic—made by humans.

State of things

Elements are made up of tiny particles called atoms. Elements can exist in three states—solid, liquid, and gas. An element may change its state when the temperature or pressure alters.

A few elements change from solid to gas, and vice versa, without becoming liquid first.

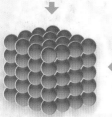

solid

A solid has a fixed, rigid shape. It will not flow or spread out. There are 101 elements that are solid at room temperature.

liquid

A liquid can flow. It changes shape to fit its container. Only bromine and mercury are liquids.

gas

A gas can also flow, and it will always expand to fill its container. There are 11 gaseous elements.

What is it?

Most elements are either metals or nonmetals. This chart shows you their different properties. A few elements, called metalloids, have both metal and nonmetal properties.

Property	Metal	Nonmetal
State at normal room temperature	Solid (except mercury)	Solid, liquid, or gas
Appearance: shiny or not shiny?	Shiny	Not shiny
Good or poor conductor of heat and electricity?	Good	Poor
Can it be beaten or stretched into shape without breaking?	Yes	No

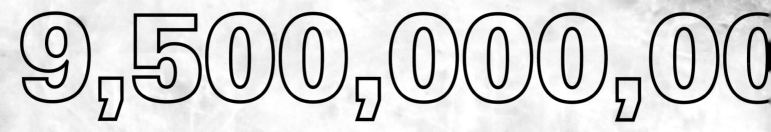

9,500,000,00

Making new substances

Elements can react, or combine, with one another to make new substances called compounds. Almost all the things around you right now are compounds. The properties of a compound can be very different from those of the elements from which it is made.

Making table salt
The elements sodium and chlorine combine to form the compound sodium chloride—table salt.

sodium

A shiny, soft metal, sodium reacts readily with other elements.

chlorine

Chlorine is a greenish gas that is poisonous in large quantities.

sodium chloride

Sodium chloride is an edible compound of white crystals.

Chemical reactions

Interactions between elements are called chemical reactions. Elements that are more prone than others to form new compounds are said to be reactive. Those that are less likely to interact are unreactive.

Reactive oxygen
Burning is a type of reaction between a substance and oxygen in the air, which releases lots of heat.

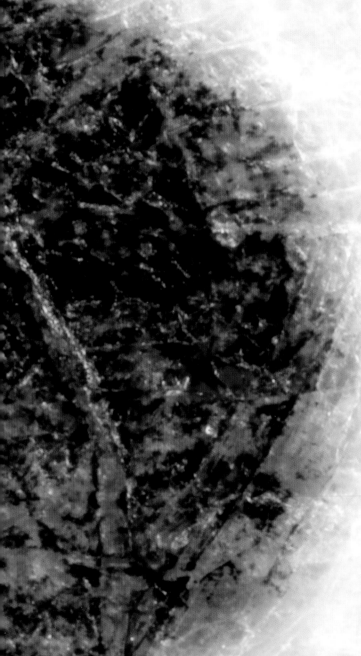

Period element
A period printed in black ink—like the magnified one shown here—is made up mostly of atoms of the element carbon.

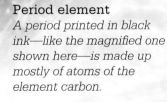

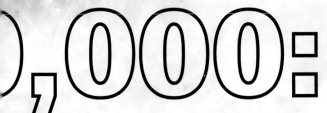

),000: **the number of atoms in a normal-size period found in a daily newspaper**

Everyday elements

Don't be fooled into thinking that elements are found only in laboratories—they're the stuff of daily life! We use them for every product we make. Cars show how we can combine the qualities of different elements for effective results.

PVC bodywork
Carbon, hydrogen, and chlorine go into PVC plastic.

Headlight
Halogen headlights are filled with mercury vapor and xenon gas.

Early cars

From the first models, steel (a mixture of iron and a little carbon) took the lead role in cars. Steel is hard, strong, and easy to shape.

Ford Model T (1908–1927)
This early car was made mostly of steel, iron, and wood.

Radiator grill
PVC is molded into complex shapes to make grills, fenders, and rearview mirrors.

Engine
Steel with vanadium added (to make it extra-tough) is used for the engine.

Upholstery
Plastics are used for interior fittings.

Perfect properties

Today's cars contain a wide range of elements and compounds. Many compounds are metallic, and metal mixtures called alloys are also used. Plastics (compounds of hydrogen, carbon, nitrogen, oxygen, and other elements) feature strongly.

Radiator
Steel fins conduct heat away from the engine.

Electric motor/generator
This uses magnets made with neodymium.

Brake disc
Hard gray steel forms the discs that stop the car.

Wheel
Magnesium alloy wheels are incredibly light—but also flammable!

Spring
Super-resistant low-carbon steel is used for the springs.

Catalytic converter
Precious metals are used in the catalytic converter (see opposite page).

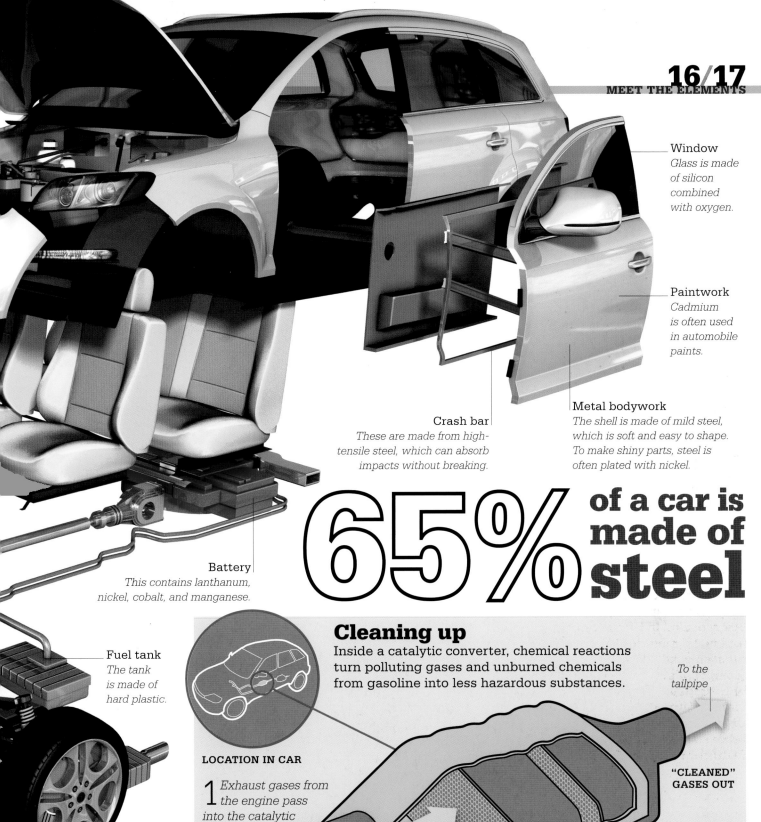

Window
Glass is made of silicon combined with oxygen.

Paintwork
Cadmium is often used in automobile paints.

Metal bodywork
The shell is made of mild steel, which is soft and easy to shape. To make shiny parts, steel is often plated with nickel.

Crash bar
These are made from high-tensile steel, which can absorb impacts without breaking.

Battery
This contains lanthanum, nickel, cobalt, and manganese.

65% of a car is made of steel

Fuel tank
The tank is made of hard plastic.

Rubber tire
Rubber is mainly carbon and hydrogen. In tires, it is stiffened with sulfur and strengthened with steel wires.

Cleaning up
Inside a catalytic converter, chemical reactions turn polluting gases and unburned chemicals from gasoline into less hazardous substances.

To the tailpipe

LOCATION IN CAR

1 *Exhaust gases from the engine pass into the catalytic converter, or "cat."*

"CLEANED" GASES OUT

"DIRTY" EXHAUST GASES IN

Ceramic filter has a thin coating of precious metals.

2 *Precious metals in the cat's ceramic filter, such as rhodium, platinum, and palladium, help the cleaning reactions take place.*

3 *Having passed through the filter, the emissions from the tailpipe are less harmful to people and the environment.*

Electron shells
Electrons travel in certain fixed orbits, known as shells. These surround the nucleus like the layers of an onion.

Electrons
These have a negative electric charge and cancel the protons' positive charge, making the atom electrically neutral.

Protons
These have a positive electric charge.

Neutrons
These particles have no electric charge.

A trip inside an atom
The number of protons and the number of electrons in an atom are the same, but the electrons whiz around so fast, it's hard to know where they are! The number of neutrons can vary. This is a beryllium atom. It has four protons. It also has four neutrons and four electrons.

Every single thing in the Universe, including human beings, is made of tiny particles called atoms. Pure elements contain atoms of only one type. Compounds (see page 15) are combinations of more than one kind of atom, joined in units called molecules.

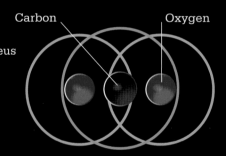

Mass of protons

Electron

PLUM PUDDING MODEL (1904)

99.9%
of an atom's mass is in its nucleus

Getting the look
Scientists once thought that atoms might be all kinds of strange shapes. J. J. Thomson (1856–1940) suggested this "plum pudding" shape, in which the electrons were embedded in a mass of protons.

Atoms and elements
Atoms are made of even smaller stuff. A nucleus, or central core, contains protons and neutrons. Electrons orbit the nucleus. All atoms of the same element have an identical number of protons.

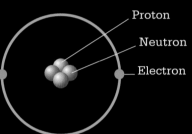

Proton

Neutron

Electron

Simple helium
Helium has simple atoms with two protons and two electrons. Helium is one of the most common elements in the Universe.

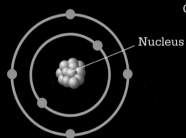

Nucleus

More complex carbon
A carbon atom has six protons and six electrons. Atoms can "steal" or "share" electrons to form bonds with other atoms.

Carbon

Oxygen

Molecules
Carbon dioxide is a compound of the elements carbon and oxygen. Its molecules have one carbon atom bonded (linked) to two oxygen atoms.

Smaller and smaller
There are even smaller particles than protons and neutrons. Machines called particle accelerators smash protons together at high speed, and scientists study the new particles that form during such collisions.

A real smasher
This is part of the world's largest particle accelerator, the Large Hadron Collider in Switzerland.

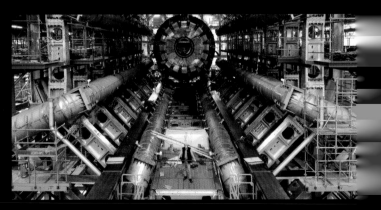

7,000,000,000,000,000,000,000,000,000:
the number of atoms in an average human

Making elements

The story of the elements goes back to the beginning of time itself. The first three elements—the light gases hydrogen and helium and the metal lithium—were created soon after our Universe sprang into existence.

From the stars

Many scientists think that the Universe began about 13.7 billion years ago in an event called the Big Bang. This produced hydrogen, helium, and lithium. All the other elements formed much later, inside stars.

1 Big Bang
This explosion was probably the beginning of everything—time, space, and all the matter in the Universe. Within half an hour, single protons formed hydrogen nuclei, and two protons and two neutrons joined together to form helium nuclei.

5 New worlds
Every time a star is formed and later dies, a cloud of stardust containing the elements is created, and new stars and planets form out of the debris of the supernova. Rare and heavy elements are carried to planets around the Universe, such as Earth, by meteorites.

99%
of everything in the Universe is just two elements —hydrogen and helium

they come from?]

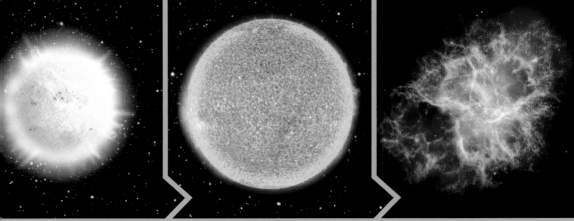

More here

George's Cosmic Treasure Hunt by Lucy and Stephen Hawking
The Hitchhiker's Guide to the Galaxy by Douglas Adams

Big Bang Universe
Kepler's Supernova
Milky Way **Crab Nebula**
Meteorite ALH84001 from Mars

2 Birth of a star
Hydrogen atoms form vast clouds, called nebulae. These collapse, getting hotter and making new stars form. The huge amount of energy released makes the stars shine brightly.

3 Burned out
A star fuses hydrogen atoms together to make helium. When it runs out of hydrogen, it starts fusing helium to form carbon. This process continues, making heavier elements up to iron.

4 Supernova
At the end of its life, a massive star explodes as a supernova. The explosion's extreme temperature and pressure allow gold, uranium, and other elements heavier than iron to form.

Look at the stars through a telescope and see new elements in the making!

Visit the Smithsonian National Air and Space Museum in Washington, D.C. Check out the Griffith Observatory in Los Angeles, CA.

fusion: the process that creates a new element by joining the nuclei of atoms.

meteorite: a piece of space rock that lands on Earth.

nebula: a cloud of gas and dust in space.

supernova: a huge explosion that takes place when a star has used up all its fuel and collapses.

The periodic table [Sorting

The periodic table organizes all the elements according to their shared characteristics. This arrangement was devised in 1869 by Dmitri Mendeleev (see page 102), a Russian chemist. You can predict an element's "personality"—its properties and chemical behavior—from its position in the table.

A shining example

An element's atomic number shows how many protons there are in the nucleus (see page 18). Each element also has a unique symbol—normally one or two letters taken from its name.

22 — Atomic number
Ti — Symbol
TITANIUM — Element name

Elements become less metallic in this direction.

GROUPS (VERTICAL COLUMNS)

PERIODS (HORIZONTAL ROWS)

1	2	3	4	5	6	7	8	9	10
1 **H** HYDROGEN									
3 **Li** LITHIUM	4 **Be** BERYLLIUM								
11 **Na** SODIUM	12 **Mg** MAGNESIUM								
19 **K** POTASSIUM	20 **Ca** CALCIUM	21 **Sc** SCANDIUM	22 **Ti** TITANIUM	23 **V** VANADIUM	24 **Cr** CHROMIUM	25 **Mn** MANGANESE	26 **Fe** IRON	27 **Co** COBALT	28 **Ni** NICKEL
37 **Rb** RUBIDIUM	38 **Sr** STRONTIUM	39 **Y** YTTRIUM	40 **Zr** ZIRCONIUM	41 **Nb** NIOBIUM	42 **Mo** MOLYBDENUM	43 **Tc** TECHNETIUM	44 **Ru** RUTHENIUM	45 **Rh** RHODIUM	46 **Pd** PALLADIUM
55 **Cs** CESIUM	56 **Ba** BARIUM	57–71 **La–Lu** LANTHANOIDS	72 **Hf** HAFNIUM	73 **Ta** TANTALUM	74 **W** TUNGSTEN	75 **Re** RHENIUM	76 **Os** OSMIUM	77 **Ir** IRIDIUM	78 **Pt** PLATINUM
87 **Fr** FRANCIUM	88 **Ra** RADIUM	89–103 **Ac–Lr** ACTINOIDS	104 **Rf** RUTHERFORDIUM	105 **Db** DUBNIUM	106 **Sg** SEABORGIUM	107 **Bh** BOHRIUM	108 **Hs** HASSIUM	109 **Mt** MEITNERIUM	110 **Ds** DARMSTADTIUM

Period numbers (rows): 1, 2, 3, 4, 5, 6, 7

With scandium and yttrium, the lanthanoids are together known as rare earth metals.

57 **La** LANTHANUM	58 **Ce** CERIUM	59 **Pr** PRASEODYMIUM	60 **Nd** NEODYMIUM	61 **Pm** PROMETHIUM	62 **Sm** SAMARIUM	63 **Eu** EUROPIUM
89 **Ac** ACTINIUM	90 **Th** THORIUM	91 **Pa** PROTACTINIUM	92 **U** URANIUM	93 **Np** NEPTUNIUM	94 **Pu** PLUTONIUM	95 **Am** AMERICIUM

3/4 of all known elements are metals

92 elements occur naturally on Earth, the rest are manufactured

Fluorine is the most reactive element.

Silicon is the second most abundant element in Earth's crust.

Silver is both the best conductor and the most reflective element.

13	14	15	16	17	18
					2 **He** HELIUM
5 **B** BORON	6 **C** CARBON	7 **N** NITROGEN	8 **O** OXYGEN	9 **F** FLUORINE	10 **Ne** NEON
13 **Al** ALUMINUM	14 **Si** SILICON	15 **P** PHOSPHORUS	16 **S** SULFUR	17 **Cl** CHLORINE	18 **Ar** ARGON

11	12	13	14	15	16	17	18
29 **Cu** COPPER	30 **Zn** ZINC	31 **Ga** GALLIUM	32 **Ge** GERMANIUM	33 **As** ARSENIC	34 **Se** SELENIUM	35 **Br** BROMINE	36 **Kr** KRYPTON
47 **Ag** SILVER	48 **Cd** CADMIUM	49 **In** INDIUM	50 **Sn** TIN	51 **Sb** ANTIMONY	52 **Te** TELLURIUM	53 **I** IODINE	54 **Xe** XENON
79 **Au** GOLD	80 **Hg** MERCURY	81 **Tl** THALLIUM	82 **Pb** LEAD	83 **Bi** BISMUTH	84 **Po** POLONIUM	85 **At** ASTATINE	86 **Rn** RADON
111 **Rg** ROENTGENIUM	112 **Cn** COPERNICIUM		114 **Uuq** UNUNQUADIUM		116 **Uuh** UNUNHEXIUM		

Other elements
Elements 113, 115, 117, and 118 are awaiting official recognition and naming.

64 **Gd** GADOLINIUM	65 **Tb** TERBIUM	66 **Dy** DYSPROSIUM	67 **Ho** HOLMIUM	68 **Er** ERBIUM	69 **Tm** THULIUM	70 **Yb** YTTERBIUM	71 **Lu** LUTETIUM
96 **Cm** CURIUM	97 **Bk** BERKELIUM	98 **Cf** CALIFORNIUM	99 **Es** EINSTEINIUM	100 **Fm** FERMIUM	101 **Md** MENDELEVIUM	102 **No** NOBELIUM	103 **Lr** LAWRENCIUM

Team talk

The groups, or vertical columns, are families of elements that react in similar ways. Generally, the elements in a group become more reactive toward the bottom. Sometimes, similarities are also shared across neighboring groups, forming larger teams of related elements.

Alkali metals
Soft, shiny, and extremely reactive metals.

Alkaline earth metals
Silvery-white reactive metals that form minerals.

Transition metals
Tough, versatile metals that are easy to shape.

Poor metals
Soft metals with some nonmetal properties.

Metalloids
These have both metal and nonmetal properties.

Nonmetals
Gases and solids with differing chemistry.

Halogens
A group of reactive elements, also called salt-formers.

Noble gases
Generally unreactive, colorless, and odorless.

Lanthanoids
Reactive metals with a similar chemistry.

Actinoids
Many of these are made in nuclear reactors.

The periodic table lays out the elements in order of increasing atomic number. Solid metal elements fill up most of the table, while nonmetals and gases cluster on the right-hand side. Not all the elements are pictured in this gallery. Some elements exist only briefly before they decay by radioactivity (see pages 64–65), so it is not possible to photograph them.

H 1 HYDROGEN	

Li 3  LITHIUM	**Be** 4 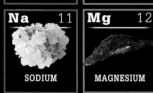 BERYLLIUM
Na 11 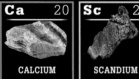 SODIUM	**Mg** 12 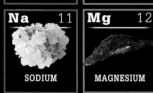 MAGNESIUM

K 19	**Ca** 20	**Sc** 21	**Ti** 22	**V** 23	**Cr** 24	**Mn** 25	**Fe** 26	**Co** 27
POTASSIUM	CALCIUM	SCANDIUM	TITANIUM	VANADIUM	CHROMIUM	MANGANESE	IRON	COBALT
Rb 37	**Sr** 38	**Y** 39	**Zr** 40	**Nb** 41	**Mo** 42	**Tc** 43	**Ru** 44	**Rh** 45
RUBIDIUM	STRONTIUM	YTTRIUM	ZIRCONIUM	NIOBIUM	MOLYBDENUM	TECHNETIUM	RUTHENIUM	RHODIUM
Cs 55	**Ba** 56	57–71 **La–Lu**	**Hf** 72	**Ta** 73	**W** 74	**Re** 75	**Os** 76	**Ir** 77
CESIUM	BARIUM	LANTHANOIDS	HAFNIUM	TANTALUM	TUNGSTEN	RHENIUM	OSMIUM	IRIDIUM
Fr 87	**Ra** 88	89–103 **Ac–Lr**	104 **Rf**	105 **Db**	106 **Sg**	107 **Bh**	108 **Hs**	109 **Mt**
FRANCIUM	RADIUM	ACTINOIDS	RUTHERFORDIUM	DUBNIUM	SEABORGIUM	BOHRIUM	HASSIUM	MEITNERIUM

Bismuth (83)
When this element cools from a molten state, it forms unusual square spiral shapes.

La 57	**Ce** 58	**Pr** 59	**Nd** 60	**Pm** 61	**Sm** 62
LANTHANUM	CERIUM	PRASEODYMIUM	NEODYMIUM	PROMETHIUM	SAMARIUM
Ac 89	**Th** 90	**Pa** 91	**U** 92	93 **Np**	**Pu** 94
ACTINIUM	THORIUM	PROTACTINIUM	URANIUM	NEPTUNIUM	PLUTONIUM

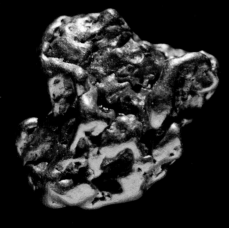

Gold (79)

Many elements are extremely reactive, meaning that they combine readily with other elements. Precious metals, such as gold, are both rare and highly unreactive.

Some gases are naturally colorless but glow when electricity passes through them.

He	2

HELIUM

B	5

BORON

C	6

CARBON

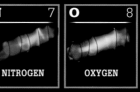

N	7

NITROGEN

O	8

OXYGEN

F	9

FLUORINE

Ne	10

NEON

Al	13

ALUMINUM

Si	14

SILICON

P	15

PHOSPHORUS

S	16

SULFUR

Cl	17

CHLORINE

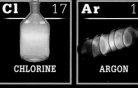

Ar	18

ARGON

Ni	28

NICKEL

Cu	29

COPPER

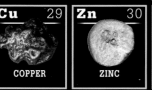

Zn	30

ZINC

Ga	31

GALLIUM

Ge	32

GERMANIUM

As	33

ARSENIC

Se	34

SELENIUM

Br	35

BROMINE

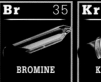

Kr	36

KRYPTON

Pd	46

PALLADIUM

Ag	47

SILVER

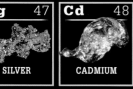

Cd	48

CADMIUM

In	49

INDIUM

Sn	50

TIN

Sb	51

ANTIMONY

Te	52

TELLURIUM

I	53

IODINE

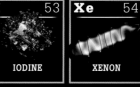

Xe	54

XENON

Pt	78

PLATINUM

Au	79

GOLD

Hg	80

MERCURY

Tl	81

THALLIUM

Pb	82

LEAD

Bi	83

BISMUTH

Po	84

POLONIUM

At	85

ASTATINE

Rn	86

RADON

110

Ds

DARMSTADTIUM

111

Rg

ROENTGENIUM

112

Cn

COPERNICIUM

114

Uuq

UNUNQUADIUM

116

Uuh

UNUNHEXIUM

Other elements
Elements 113, 115, 117, and 118 are awaiting official recognition.

Eu	63

EUROPIUM

Gd	64

GADOLINIUM

Tb	65

TERBIUM

Dy	66

DYSPROSIUM

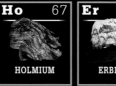

Ho	67

HOLMIUM

Er	68

ERBIUM

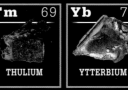

Tm	69

THULIUM

Yb	70

YTTERBIUM

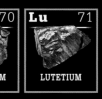

Lu	71

LUTETIUM

Am	95

AMERICIUM

96

Cm

CURIUM

97

Bk

BERKELIUM

98

Cf

CALIFORNIUM

99

Es

EINSTEINIUM

100

Fm

FERMIUM

101

Md

MENDELEVIUM

102

No

NOBELIUM

103

Lr

LAWRENCIUM

Fiery &
me

* Which elements explode when mixed with water?

* Why does an airship float?

* What gives fireworks their spectacular colors?

fizzing tals

Fiery & fizzing metals

Hydrogen sits right at the top of the periodic table. It has the simplest atoms of all, consisting of a single electron orbiting a single proton. Along with the two groups of light, reactive metals, hydrogen—a highly explosive gas—ensures that things begin with a bang!

Alkali metals (shown in red)

Alkaline earth metals (pink)

Hotheaded elements

The alkali metals of Group 1 include cesium and francium, the most reactive of all the metal elements. The Group 1 metals form compounds easily and react aggressively with water. The alkaline earth metals of Group 2 are also reactive, but less so than the alkali metals. Hydrogen, a gas, also has a fiery personality and burns readily.

An average human body
weighing 154 lbs. (70 kg) contains

15.4 lbs. (7 kg) **hydrogen**

2.2 lbs. (1 kg) **calcium**

5 oz. (140 g) **potassium**

3.5 oz. (100 g) **sodium**

1.2 oz. (35 g) **magnesium**

Sodium and water

This experiment shows what happens when sodium, a Group 1 alkali metal, comes into contact with water. It was performed under laboratory conditions.

WARNING! DON'T
TRY THIS AT HOME

1 *A piece of sodium is placed on filter paper in a water bath. You only need a small lump . . .*

2 *. . . because as soon as the water soaks through the filter paper, the reaction begins!*

3 *The reaction is violent. Hydrogen gas is released from the water and ignites due to the heat of the reaction.*

Alkali metals [The wildest

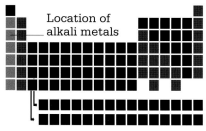

Location of alkali metals

PERIODIC TABLE

The highly reactive Group 1 elements all react vigorously with water. They never occur naturally by themselves, and they form stable compounds, called salts, with nonmetals. The alkali metals are lightweight and soft enough to cut with a knife.

Lithium

| 3 |
| Li |
| LITHIUM |

This is the lightest of all the metals. It is often combined with other metals to form light alloys for making aircraft and rocket parts. Lithium is also used in some types of battery.

What it is	A silvery-white metal
Melting point	356.97°F (180.54°C)
Boiling point	2,448°F (1,342°C)

CELL PHONE LITHIUM–ION BATTERIES

Sodium

| 11 |
| Na |
| SODIUM |

We eat sodium in the form of sodium chloride (a compound of sodium and chlorine), or table salt. Sodium is essential to the human body, because it helps transmit nerve signals.

What it is	A silvery-gray metal
Melting point	207.9°F (97.72°C)
Boiling point	1,621°F (883°C)

HALITE (ROCK SALT)

GPS SCREEN IN CAR

Rubidium

| 37 |
| Rb |
| RUBIDIUM |

This element is barely solid at normal room temperature. Rubidium is used in the devices that control TVs, cell phones, and GPS (satellite navigation) signals.

What it is	A gray-white metal
Melting point	102.76°F (39.31°C)
Boiling point	1,270°F (688°C)

33.7%: the salt content of the Dead Sea

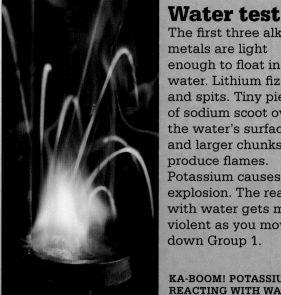

Water test

The first three alkali metals are light enough to float in water. Lithium fizzes and spits. Tiny pieces of sodium scoot over the water's surface, and larger chunks produce flames. Potassium causes an explosion. The reaction with water gets more violent as you move down Group 1.

KA-BOOM! POTASSIUM REACTING WITH WATER

Francium

| 87 |
| Fr |
| FRANCIUM |

This metal doesn't hang around; it has a half-life of 22 minutes. In the time it takes to cook a pizza, half of its atoms decay, sending out nuclear radiation (see pages 64–65).

What it is	A radioactive metal
Predicted melting point	80°F (27°C)
Predicted boiling point	1,250°F (677°C)

URANITE (A MINERAL CONTAINING FRANCIUM)

Cesium

| 55 |
| Cs |
| CESIUM |

This gold-tinged element is the most reactive metal, and it also has the largest atoms. It is found in superaccurate atomic clocks. These keep time by detecting regular changes in cesium atoms.

What it is	A soft, silvery-gold metal
Melting point	83.19°F (28.44°C)
Boiling point	1,240°F (671°C)

Tick tock, atomic clock
Atomic clocks are accurate to within one second for a million years!

bunch]

CRYSTALS OF POTASSIUM
DICHROMATE (A COMPOUND
OF POTASSIUM, CHROMIUM,
AND OXYGEN)

More here

salt Humphry Davy
GPS atomic clock
flame tests nerve signals
radioactivity

Get experimenting!
Salt water is denser than
freshwater. You can test
this yourself. Gently lower
an egg into a glass half full
of tap water and watch
what happens. Next, stir
6–10 tablespoons of salt
into the water until
it dissolves. Then put the
egg in the water again.
What happens now?

alloy: a metallic
mixture made of two
or more metal elements.

half-life: the time it takes
for half the atoms in a
sample of a radioactive
element to decay.

radioactive decay:
the natural breakup
of atomic nuclei in
radioactive elements.

Potassium

19
K
POTASSIUM

Even more reactive than
sodium, potassium burns
with a lilac flame. Like sodium,
it helps send nerve signals in the
body—so eat lots of potassium-rich
foods, such as bananas!

What it is	A silvery-gray metal
Melting point	146.08°F (63.38°C)
Boiling point	1,398°F (759°C)
Special features	Explodes on contact with water

Hydrogen The chart topper

Element Profile

Name	Hydrogen
Symbol	H
Atomic number	1
What it is	A colorless, odorless gas
Melting point	−434.45°F (−259.14°C)
Boiling point	−423.17°F (−252.87°C)
Special features	14 times lighter than air; explosive

1
H
HYDROGEN

Hydrogen is number one in so many ways! This colorless gas has the atomic number 1 (see page 22), and it starts off the periodic table. Hydrogen was the first element to exist, and it is the lightest and most common of all the elements.

Fuel of the stars

The element that fuels stars such as our Sun is hydrogen. Inside the Sun's core, hydrogen atoms combine to form helium atoms in a process called nuclear fusion (see pages 20–21). This process gives off energy that travels through space to heat and light our world.

Solar flare
A solar flare is an explosion on the Sun's surface that blasts a streamer of superhot hydrogen into space.

The Sun burns

683

million tons of hydrogen every second

Neon 0.13%
Carbon 0.46%
Oxygen 1.04%
Everything else 0.37%
Helium 24%
Hydrogen 74%

Composition of the Universe
Hydrogen is the most common element in the Universe. Second place goes to helium. Together, the other 112 elements make up just 2 percent of the matter in the Universe.

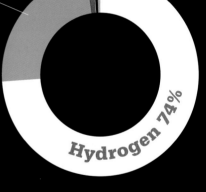

Hydrogen giants
Some giant planets are made mostly of hydrogen. Saturn's solid core is wrapped in layers of solid and liquid hydrogen, and 93 percent of its atmosphere is hydrogen gas.

Water

There is almost no hydrogen gas on Earth, because it is so light that it rises through the atmosphere and escapes into space. But hydrogen combined with oxygen, as the compound water, covers 71 percent of the planet's surface.

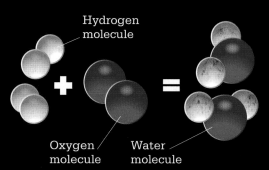

Hydrogen molecule

Oxygen molecule

Water molecule

What's in water?
Each water molecule is made of one oxygen (O) atom joined to two hydrogen (H) atoms. So, scientifically, water is written as "H_2O."

Producing hydrogen

Solar-power towers (right) use the Sun's energy to split water molecules and release hydrogen. It takes searing temperatures of 2,192°F (1,200°C) to achieve this.

Hydrosol-II, Spain

Solar tower
Mirrors focus sunlight onto a central tower to generate intense heat.

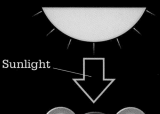

Sunlight

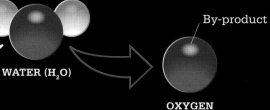

WATER (H_2O)

By-product

OXYGEN

HYDROGEN

Fuel burned

Energy

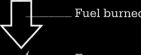

Power from hydrogen
When hydrogen burns, it releases lots of energy. This energy can be used to power vehicles, or it can be converted into electricity. Burning hydrogen is a good alternative to using up Earth's oil supplies, and it doesn't cause pollution.

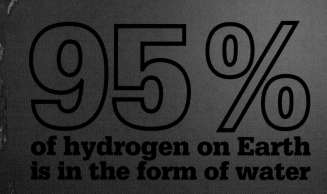

95%
of hydrogen on Earth is in the form of water

Hindenburg explodes!

Hydrogen is 14 times lighter than air, so things filled with hydrogen will rise. In the 1930s, hydrogen was used inside airships such as the *Hindenburg*, which carried passengers between Europe and the United States. But on May 6, 1937, disaster struck. The *Hindenburg* was docking at its mooring mast when it caught fire. The gas inside quickly demonstrated another of hydrogen's key characteristics—it is very explosive. The resulting fireball wrecked the airship and killed 36 people.

7:00PM — *Hindenburg approaches Lakehurst Naval Station in New Jersey, where it is due to dock.*

7:21PM — *The crew throws mooring ropes toward the mooring mast.*

7:24PM — *The ground crew spots part of the airship's outer fabric fluttering, as if gas is leaking out.*

7:25PM — *Hindenburg catches fire and the hydrogen inside quickly ignites.*

The rear of the airship explodes in a gigantic fireball and crashes to the ground.

A burst of flames shoots out of the nose, killing nine of the crew.

The exploding hydrogen gas shoots upward because it is lighter than air, so, amazingly, many passengers traveling in the gondola under the airship survive.

The front of the airship crashes.

7:27PM — *The hydrogen burns up in just 90 seconds. Hindenburg is reduced to twisted wreckage in 34 seconds. The diesel fuel for the airship's propellers blazes for hours.*

"It burst into flames, and it's falling, it's crashing! It's crashing terrible!

Alkaline earth metals [The

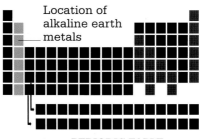
Location of alkaline earth metals

PERIODIC TABLE

The metals in this group are exceptionally light, yet strong, too, which is why they are often added to alloys. Although not as reactive as the alkali metals (pages 30–31), they combine easily with oxygen, forming minerals that are found in Earth's crust.

Magnesium
12 Mg MAGNESIUM

Superlight magnesium alloys are used to reduce weight in the engines of racing cars, fast jets, and rockets. Magnesium burns with a brilliant white flame. Once alight, it is nearly impossible to extinguish.

What it is	A silvery-white metal
Melting point	1,202°F (650°C)
Boiling point	1,994°F (1,090°C)

Magnesium crystals
Magnesium can be extracted from many minerals, and also from seawater.

Strontium
38 Sr STRONTIUM

When exposed to the air, this silvery metal reacts with oxygen and quickly turns yellowish. Strontium burns with a bright red flame, and it is often used in fireworks.

Mayday!
The red flare of burning strontium is an internationally recognized distress signal.

What it is	A soft silvery metal
Melting point	1,431°F (777°C)
Boiling point	2,520°F (1,382°C)

Radium
88 Ra RADIUM

Radioactive radium was once used to make luminous paint for instrument dials and watch hands. It was thought to be good for the health and was even added to water and toothpaste—until people began dying of radiation-related illnesses.

What it is	A radioactive white metal
Melting point	1,292°F (700°C)
Boiling point	3,159°F (1,737°C)

5th most common element in the oceans: magnesium

Autunite
Radium occurs in tiny amounts in ores such as autunite and uraninite.

Barium
56 Ba BARIUM

The compound barium sulfate—barium combined with sulfur and oxygen—is given to people with stomach disorders as a "barium meal." Once swallowed, the barium shows up on X-ray photographs, allowing doctors to see what's going on in the patient's digestive system.

What it is	A silvery-gray metal
Melting point	1,341°F (727°C)
Boiling point	3,398°F (1,870°C)

Here's looking at you!
A barium meal is used to look at your guts. The heavy barium blocks the path of X-rays, showing up as dark areas in this image.

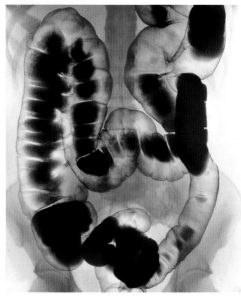

7.7 tons of ore is needed to produce just 0.035 oz. (1 g) of radium

Other alkaline earth metals: Calcium (Ca)

4
Be
BERYLLIUM

Beryllium

Tools made from beryllium-copper alloys are hard and do not create sparks when they strike a surface. They are used in places where preventing fire is crucial, such as in oil refineries.

What it is	A silvery-white metal
Melting point	2,349°F (1,287°C)
Boiling point	4,476°F (2,469°C)
Special features	Hard enough to scratch glass; among the most toxic elements

Green gems

The mineral beryl is one of the beryllium ores—the other is bertrandite. Crystals of green beryl are used to make gemstones known as emeralds.

Pure beryl is colorless. The green of emeralds is usually the result of chromium impurities.

Calcium [The builder]

20
Ca
CALCIUM

Calcium is a shiny metal, but it is seldom seen in this form because it easily joins with other elements. It is an element that builds, and its strong compounds make great construction materials—for people as well as for buildings!

Element profile

Name	Calcium
Symbol	Ca
Atomic number	20
What it is	A soft, shiny metal
Melting point	1,548°F (842°C)
Boiling point	2,703°F (1,484°C)
Special features	Very reactive; forms compounds readily; dissolves in water

Hard shells

Some sea creatures take dissolved calcium from the water and use it to make protective shells. The shells remain long after the animal dies. Some shells turn into fossils.

Stunning shells
Seashells come in a variety of shapes and sizes, often with amazing patterns and colors.

Miracle mineral

When a bone breaks, a blood clot forms at the site, and stringy fibers grow to link the broken ends. Bone-building cells called osteoblasts lay down layers of calcium minerals, from which new bone begins to form.

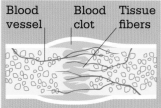

Blood vessel   Blood clot   Tissue fibers

New bone forming

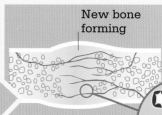

Bridging the gap
New blood vessels and tissue fibers grow across the break in the bone.

Fixing the break
Osteoblasts deposit calcium minerals, which turn into bone.

OSTEOBLASTS

Bone health

Your body contains about 2.2 pounds (1 kilogram) of calcium, most of which is in your bones as calcium phosphate (a compound of calcium, oxygen, and phosphorus). A calcium-rich diet helps maintain healthy bones.

Teeth
The minerals that make up this fearsome set of gnashers are calcium compounds.

Bones
Your bony skeleton is light, strong, and flexible. It encases your brain and keeps you upright.

Teeth are protected by a hard, calcium-based coating called enamel.

Construction king

Limestone is a form of calcium carbonate (calcium combined with carbon and oxygen). Solid yet relatively easy to cut, it has been used for building since ancient times. Today, limestone is an ingredient in concrete.

Ancient pyramids
Made of limestone slabs, Egypt's pyramids were faced with blocks polished to a brilliant white shine.

Concrete giant
The Pentagon was built with 435,000 cubic yards (333,000 cubic meters) of steel-reinforced concrete.

Calcium in space

Calcium is made inside stars (see pages 20–21). When a star explodes as a supernova, it scatters the calcium into space.

X-RAY PHOTO SHOWING ONLY THE CALCIUM IN CASSIOPEIA A

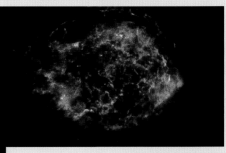

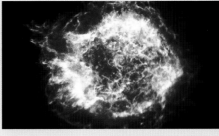

X-RAY PHOTO OF CASSIOPEIA A

Cassiopeia A
The amount of calcium in Cassiopeia A, the remains of a dead star, is equal to 1,100 times the mass of Earth.

Each year, enough concrete to fill
400,000
Olympic swimming pools is made

Firework colors

This fireworks display over Washington, D.C., gets its bright colors from a range of alkali and transition-metal compounds that are added to the explosive mixture. Strontium and lithium produce vivid reds as they burn, barium compounds make green, and copper creates blue. Yellow comes from sodium, while white flashes are made using aluminum, magnesium, titanium, and zirconium powders.

Mains
me

* What is Earth made of?

* How are astronauts shielded from the Sun?

* Which paint used by artists was a rat killer?

tream

tals

Mainstream metals

These shiny substances make up the vast majority of elements in the periodic table. The transition metals are generally malleable (able to be shaped without breaking), can be mixed to make alloys, and will conduct electricity. They are also the best conductors of heat—that's why they are cold to the touch, since they take heat away from your hand. Many metals are magnetic.

WARNING! DON'T TRY THIS AT HOME

Types of metal

Transition metals form the main body of the periodic table. They are strong and hard, with high melting points. The poor metals, to the right, have lower melting points and are softer. The lanthanoids are all very similar and are usually set apart from the main block of metals. The same is true of the actinoids. Metalloids have both metallic and nonmetallic properties.

Aluminum and iron oxide

In this chemical reaction, carried out under strict laboratory conditions, the poor metal aluminum frees the transition metal iron from iron oxide (a compound of iron and oxygen).

1 *Powdered iron oxide and aluminum are mixed in a glass beaker. As a precaution, the beaker is placed in a cast-iron vessel filled with sand. It's a dangerous combination!*

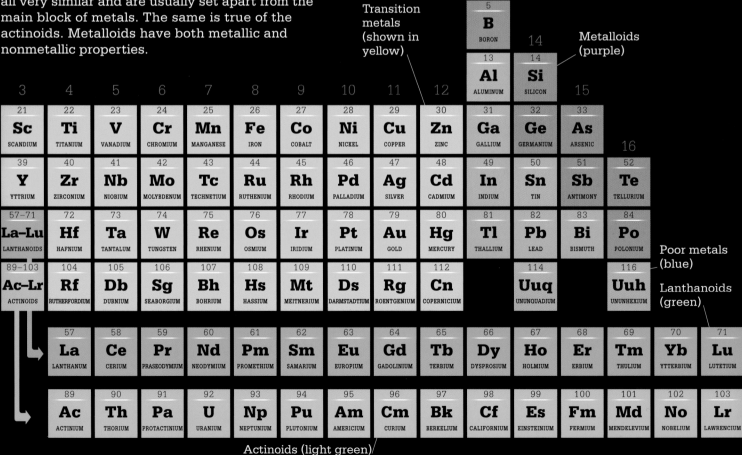

Transition metals (shown in yellow)

Metalloids (purple)

Poor metals (blue)

Lanthanoids (green)

Actinoids (light green)

13		
5 **B** BORON		
13 **Al** ALUMINUM	14 **Si** SILICON	

	3	4	5	6	7	8	9	10	11	12	13	14	15	16
	21 **Sc** SCANDIUM	22 **Ti** TITANIUM	23 **V** VANADIUM	24 **Cr** CHROMIUM	25 **Mn** MANGANESE	26 **Fe** IRON	27 **Co** COBALT	28 **Ni** NICKEL	29 **Cu** COPPER	30 **Zn** ZINC	31 **Ga** GALLIUM	32 **Ge** GERMANIUM	33 **As** ARSENIC	
	39 **Y** YTTRIUM	40 **Zr** ZIRCONIUM	41 **Nb** NIOBIUM	42 **Mo** MOLYBDENUM	43 **Tc** TECHNETIUM	44 **Ru** RUTHENIUM	45 **Rh** RHODIUM	46 **Pd** PALLADIUM	47 **Ag** SILVER	48 **Cd** CADMIUM	49 **In** INDIUM	50 **Sn** TIN	51 **Sb** ANTIMONY	52 **Te** TELLURIUM
	57–71 **La–Lu** LANTHANOIDS	72 **Hf** HAFNIUM	73 **Ta** TANTALUM	74 **W** TUNGSTEN	75 **Re** RHENIUM	76 **Os** OSMIUM	77 **Ir** IRIDIUM	78 **Pt** PLATINUM	79 **Au** GOLD	80 **Hg** MERCURY	81 **Tl** THALLIUM	82 **Pb** LEAD	83 **Bi** BISMUTH	84 **Po** POLONIUM
	89–103 **Ac–Lr** ACTINOIDS	104 **Rf** RUTHERFORDIUM	105 **Db** DUBNIUM	106 **Sg** SEABORGIUM	107 **Bh** BOHRIUM	108 **Hs** HASSIUM	109 **Mt** MEITNERIUM	110 **Ds** DARMSTADTIUM	111 **Rg** ROENTGENIUM	112 **Cn** COPERNICIUM		114 **Uuq** UNUNQUADIUM		116 **Uuh** UNUNHEXIUM

57 **La** LANTHANUM	58 **Ce** CERIUM	59 **Pr** PRASEODYMIUM	60 **Nd** NEODYMIUM	61 **Pm** PROMETHIUM	62 **Sm** SAMARIUM	63 **Eu** EUROPIUM	64 **Gd** GADOLINIUM	65 **Tb** TERBIUM	66 **Dy** DYSPROSIUM	67 **Ho** HOLMIUM	68 **Er** ERBIUM	69 **Tm** THULIUM	70 **Yb** YTTERBIUM	71 **Lu** LUTETIUM
89 **Ac** ACTINIUM	90 **Th** THORIUM	91 **Pa** PROTACTINIUM	92 **U** URANIUM	93 **Np** NEPTUNIUM	94 **Pu** PLUTONIUM	95 **Am** AMERICIUM	96 **Cm** CURIUM	97 **Bk** BERKELIUM	98 **Cf** CALIFORNIUM	99 **Es** EINSTEINIUM	100 **Fm** FERMIUM	101 **Md** MENDELEVIUM	102 **No** NOBELIUM	103 **Lr** LAWRENCIUM

3 The reaction produces molten iron, which eats right through the bottom of the beaker and even fuses the sand in the pot. Scary stuff!

2 A magnesium ribbon is lit to ignite the powdered metal mixture. As the temperature soars to 4,530°F (2,500°C), the aluminum tears the oxygen away from the iron oxide. The whole area is showered with red-hot burning metal.

Earth [What's our rocky planet

Our planet is built like an almost-spherical layer cake, with tiers of different materials piled on top of one another. Amazingly, 90 percent of Earth is made up of just four elements—iron, oxygen, silicon, and magnesium!

Recipe for a planet

To make a rocky planet such as Earth, you need minerals. These solid substances are crystals of unreactive elements and chemical combinations of more reactive elements. Most minerals are made of a combination of oxygen and silicon.

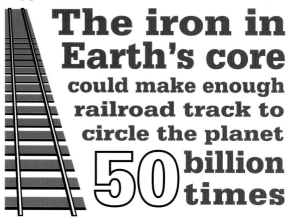

The iron in Earth's core
could make enough railroad track to circle the planet 50 billion times

Chemical copycat

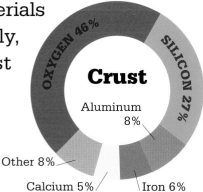

The Moon seems to be chemically identical to Earth. Scientists think that it formed when a planet-size meteor collided with Earth, knocking a large chunk off into space. In 2009, NASA's LCROSS space probe crashed a spent rocket booster into the Moon and found evidence of ice in craters at its south pole.

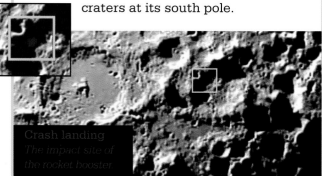

Crash landing
The impact site of the rocket booster

Composition of the crust

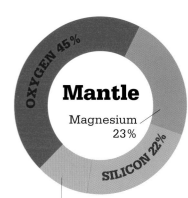

OXYGEN 46%
SILICON 27%
Crust
Aluminum 8%
Other 8%
Calcium 5%
Iron 6%

Composition of the crust
Most of the planet's oxygen is locked up in minerals in Earth's crust—the solid top layer.

OXYGEN 45%
SILICON 22%
Mantle
Magnesium 23%
Other 10%

Composition of the mantle
The mantle makes up 70 percent of Earth's volume. It is mainly oxygen-based compounds.

IRON 89%
Core
Sulfur 4.5%
Other 1%
Nickel 5.5%

Composition of the core
Heavy and dense elements are mostly found right in the core, or center, of Earth.

Atmosphere
This is where all the gassy elements—mostly nitrogen and oxygen—are found.

Surface
Nearly 71 percent of the surface is covered by water, which contains most of the hydrogen.

Crust
At 3–44 miles (5–70 km) thick, the crust is the source of all the metals and raw materials we use.

Mantle
The middle layer is 1,800 miles (2,900 km) thick and made up of oxygen, silicon, and magnesium.

Outer core
The outer core is 1,429 miles (2,300 km) thick and consists of molten iron, nickel, and sulfur.

Inner core
Earth's inner core is solid and 745 miles (1,200 km) thick. It is mostly iron and nickel.

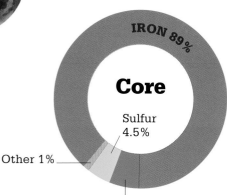

made of?]

More here

minerals crust **core** mantle **atmosphere** iron **oxygen**

Visit the Hoba Meteorite in Grootfontein, Namibia— the largest meteorite ever found and the largest known single mass of iron on Earth.

EARTH FACT FILE

Diameter:
7,926 miles (12,755 km)

Weight:
6,600 billion billion tons

Average distance from Sun:
93,000,000 miles
(150,000,000 km)

Highest point:
Mount Everest, 29,035 feet
(8,850 m)

Lowest point:
Dead Sea, 1,385 feet
(422 m) below sea level

Temperature range:
−128.6°F to 136°F
(−89.2°C to 57.8°C)

density: a measure of how heavy an object feels; the more weighty the atoms or the more tightly packed they are, the heavier the object feels.

mineral: a naturally occurring solid compound whose atoms are ordered in crystal patterns; many rocks are made of minerals.

A trip inside Earth

At first, Earth was a superhot molten ball. Heavy iron and iron-loving elements— elements that bond easily with iron—sank to the center, because they are denser. The crust is the "scum" that floated to the surface and hardened. The atmosphere contains the lightest elements, which exist as gases.

Transition metals [Movers

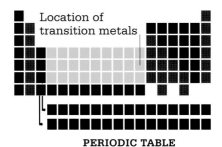

Location of transition metals

PERIODIC TABLE

Most of these metals are dense, hard, and strong, with high melting points. They conduct electricity, resist corrosion, and are easily mixed to make alloys. Transition metals also make the colored compounds used in paint pigments and fireworks.

Guggenheim Bilbao
This Spanish museum is clad in titanium panels.

Titanium
22 Ti TITANIUM

Titanium is a wonder metal, incredibly strong and amazingly hard. It is used in jet engines, ships, spacecraft, sports equipment, replacement hips, dental implants, and much more.

What it is	A shiny, very tough metal
Melting point	3,034°F (1,668°C)
Boiling point	5,949°F (3,287°C)

Silver
47 Ag SILVER

Silver conducts electricity better than any other element, including copper (see pages 54–55). It is used for high-quality electrical wires. Germs are unable to grow on silver, so it is ideal for wound dressings and medical equipment.

Cup of champions
Silver can be polished to give a beautiful shine, which makes it popular for jewelry and trophies.

What it is	A shiny silver metal
Melting point	1,763.2°F (961.78°C)
Boiling point	3,924°F (2,162°C)

Nickel
28 Ni NICKEL

Supershiny nickel does not tarnish in air. It is sometimes used to make coins. Added to alloys, it gives extra protection against rust.

What it is	A silvery, shiny, hard metal
Melting point	2,651°F (1,455°C)
Boiling point	5,275.4°F (2,913°C)

NICKEL (5-CENT) COIN

25% : proportion of nickel in a "nickel" coin

Other transition metals:
Vanadium (V); Chromium (Cr); Manganese (Mn); Iron (Fe); Cobalt (Co); Copper (Cu); Zinc (Zn); Zirconium (Zr); Niobium (Nb); Molybdenum (Mo); Technetium (Tc); Ruthenium (Ru); Rhodium (Rh); Cadmium (Cd); Hafnium (Hf); Tantalum (Ta); Rhenium (Re); Osmium (Os); Iridium (Ir); Platinum (Pt); Gold (Au)

Tungsten
74 W TUNGSTEN

Combined with carbon, tungsten forms tough tungsten carbide. This compound is used for rock drills, bulletproof armor plating, and even pen points!

TUNGSTEN CARBIDE BALLPOINT PEN NIB

What it is	A hard steel-gray metal
Melting point	6,192.6°F (3,422°C)
Boiling point	10,031°F (5,555°C)

Mercury
80 Hg MERCURY

This is the only metal that is liquid at room temperature. Mercury was used in thermometers until people realized that it is poisonous. Amalgam, a safe mercury alloy, is used in dentistry to fill cavities in teeth.

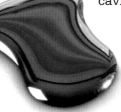

Liquid mercury
Mercury "clumps" and does not feel wet to the touch.

What it is	A slinky, silvery, liquid metal
Melting point	−37.89°F (−38.83°C)
Boiling point	674.11°F (356.73°C)

Number of years a titanium hip implant can last:

20

and shakers]

46
Pd
PALLADIUM

Palladium

This metal and its compounds are often good catalysts. Most of the palladium that is produced goes into the catalytic converters of cars (see page 17). In oil refineries, it helps to split crude oil into gas, diesel, and other useful substances (see page 89).

What it is	A shiny silvery-white metal
Melting point	2,830.82°F (1,554.9°C)
Boiling point	5,365°F (2,963°C)
Special features	Extremely rare—and expensive

MICROSCOPIC CRYSTALS OF PALLADIUM METAL

More here

The Iron Giant
by Ted Hughes

catalyst corrosion
crude oil **thermometer**
mercury barometer
pigment tungsten carbide

Visit these metal-related sites: the Chrysler Building, New York, New York; the Eiffel Tower, Paris, France; the United States Mint, Denver, Colorado

catalyst: a material that helps a chemical reaction happen. The catalyst itself is not used up or changed in the reaction.

corrosion: the chemical breakdown of the surface of a metal.

rust: a type of corrosion that happens when iron comes into contact with oxygen and water.

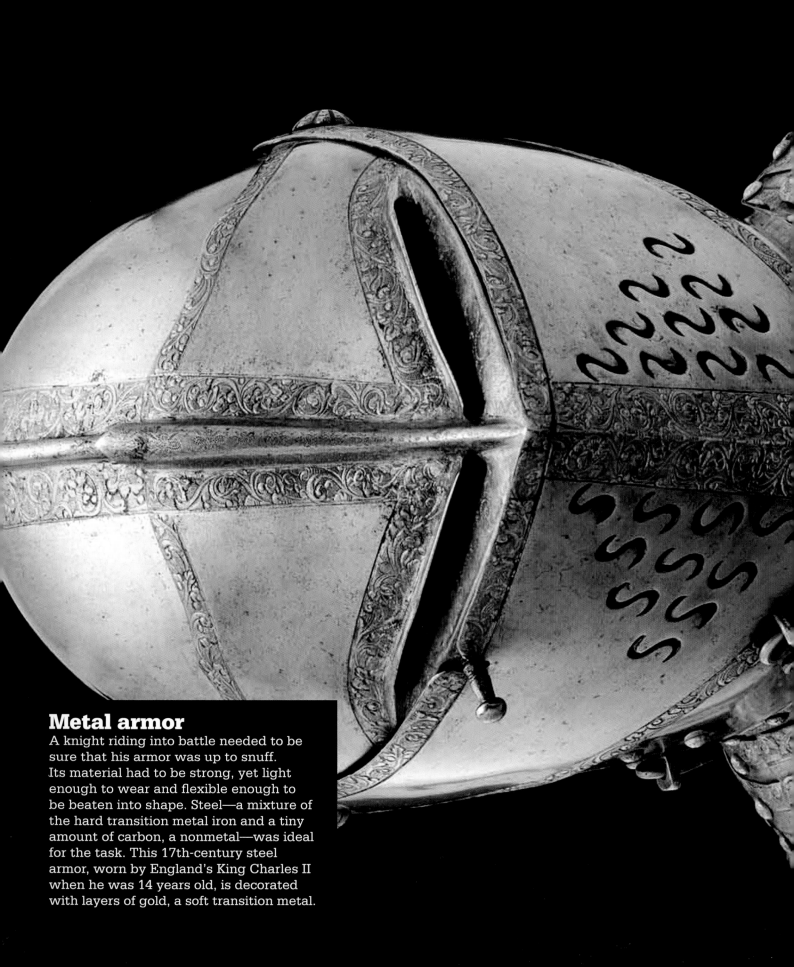

Metal armor

A knight riding into battle needed to be sure that his armor was up to snuff. Its material had to be strong, yet light enough to wear and flexible enough to be beaten into shape. Steel—a mixture of the hard transition metal iron and a tiny amount of carbon, a nonmetal—was ideal for the task. This 17th-century steel armor, worn by England's King Charles II when he was 14 years old, is decorated with layers of gold, a soft transition metal.

Gold [The king of bling]

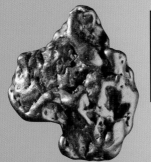

GOLD NUGGET

79
Au
GOLD

This rare and precious metal is unchanged by air, water, or time, and it keeps its gorgeous shine forever. It is the one element that everyone throughout history has desired.

Element profile

Name	Gold
Symbol	Au
Atomic number	79
What it is	A shiny yellow metal
Melting point	1,947.52°F (1,064.18°C)
Boiling point	5,173°F (2,856°C)
Special features	The only yellow metal; soft and very unreactive

FUNERAL MASK OF TUTANKHAMEN

Everlasting value

Gold's beautiful appearance and its scarcity have always made it valuable. People have been using gold as money for thousands of years, and many countries keep gold bars in their central banks to back up their currency— gold never loses its appeal.

1933 DOUBLE EAGLE, SOLD FOR $7.59 MILLION IN 2002

8,967.9	3,755.4	2,702.6	2,702.6
US	Germany	Italy	France

GOLD HOLDINGS (IN TONS)

Lasting legacy
This solid gold funeral mask was made for the burial of the Egyptian pharaoh Tutankhamen in 1323 BCE. Although it is more than 3,300 years old, it looks brand-new!

Great gold moments

ca. 1323 BCE *King Tutankhamen's golden mask is created for his burial in a tomb in the Valley of the Kings, Egypt.*

ca. 950 BCE *King Solomon builds a famous temple in Jerusalem. According to the Bible, the inside is covered with pure gold.*

58 BCE *Julius Caesar brings back enough gold from Gaul to give 200 coins to each of his soldiers and repay all of Rome's debts.*

FABERGÉ EGG

Uses of gold

About half of all the gold in the world has been made into jewelry. Some is used for decorative objects, such as the golden Easter eggs made for Czar Alexander III by Russian jeweler Carl Gustavovich Fabergé (1846–1920).

Good conduct

Gold conducts electricity well, and, more importantly, it never rusts or tarnishes. This makes it an excellent material for contacts in electronic circuits, cable connectors, and microchips.

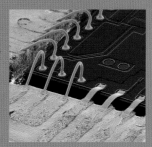

MICROCHIP

182,373 tons

—that's all the gold that has ever been found. It would make a cube with sides just 66 ft. (20 m) long.

Clear view
The astronaut is protected from glare but can still see clearly.

Precious protection
The thin coating of gold on the visor of a space helmet protects the astronaut against harmful infrared light from the Sun.

1500s *Spanish conquistadors invade the Aztec and Inca empires, seizing gold treasure and sending it back to Spain.*

1848 *The California gold rush begins at Sutter's Mill, near Sacramento. 40,000 diggers flock to California from all over the world.*

1965 *US astronaut Edward White goes on a space walk and is the first to wear a helmet with a gold-coated visor to shield him from the Sun's rays.*

Copper [Old faithful]

29
Cu
COPPER

This metal was the first to be separated from its mineral ore, about 8,000 years ago. It mixes well with other metals to form many useful alloys. Copper is a great conductor, so it is used for wires and cables in the electricity supply grid.

Element profile

Name	Copper
Symbol	Cu
Atomic number	29
What it is	A soft, malleable metal
Melting point	1,984.32°F (1,084.62°C)
Boiling point	5,301°F (2,927°C)
Special features	A superb conductor; the only reddish-orange metal

Copper reacts with the moist air over the harbor to form copper carbonate, a waterproof green coating.

The Bronze Age
By itself, copper is too soft to make long-lasting tools. About 5,000 years ago, people found that mixing copper with tin made the alloy bronze, which is much stronger.

Natural copper
Copper metal can occur naturally, but most copper is locked up in ores such as chalcopyrite and malachite.

Ancient bronze spearhead
Bronze is tough, easy to shape, and can be given a sharp edge—ideal for spears, arrows, and swords!

Blue-blooded
Spiders use copper in their blood cells to carry oxygen around their bodies. This makes their blood blue.

Tarantula spider
The redknee tarantula lives in the mountains of Mexico.

Well connected
Copper cables feed electricity from power stations to our homes. They even run under the sea, carrying currents between countries. Undersea cables also send telephone signals and link computers to the Internet.

CABLE-LAYING SHIP

Statue of Liberty
Standing at the entrance to New York Harbor is the Statue of Liberty, the world's largest copper sculpture. Copper was chosen for the statue because it is light and easy to bend, and it does not rust like iron when it comes into contact with water.

Building the statue

In 1865, French sculptor Frédéric Bartholdi was inspired to make a statue to symbolize the independence of both the French and American peoples. Work began on the 151-foot-tall (46 m) colossus in 1876.

APRIL 1876 — *Lightweight copper sheets only 0.1 inch (2.4 mm) thick are used to begin construction.*

SHAPING THE COPPER

MAY 1876 — *The right arm is completed first and sent to New York, where it is put on display in Madison Square Park.*

1878 — *The statue's head, modeled after Bartholdi's mother's, is shown at the World's Fair in Paris.*

HEAD ON SHOW IN PARIS

1880 — *Engineer Gustave Eiffel (who later designed the Eiffel Tower) devises an internal iron frame, to which the copper sections would be attached.*

1885 — *"Lady Liberty" is disassembled and shipped to the United States, but she nearly sinks during a storm en route!*

1886 — *The statue is officially dedicated.*

1984 — *Lady Liberty is given a makeover— her iron framework is replaced with corrosion-resistant stainless steel, and she gets a new set of bronze doors.*

The Statue of Liberty contains **179,000 lbs.** (81,000 kg) of copper

Radioactive elements

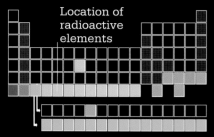

Location of radioactive elements

PERIODIC TABLE

Radioactivity is like a sickness that affects the atoms of some elements, causing their nuclei to break up. These unstable elements split apart without warning and without outside help, releasing a burst of dangerous radiation.

Atomic struggle

There is a terrific struggle going on in an atom's nucleus. Positively charged protons try to push each other apart, but a force called the strong nuclear force binds them tightly to neutrons. If the strong nuclear force breaks down, the nucleus decays (splits), sending out radiation.

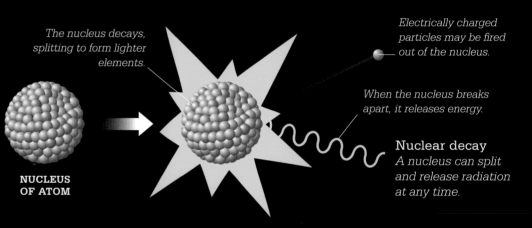

The nucleus decays, splitting to form lighter elements.

NUCLEUS OF ATOM

Electrically charged particles may be fired out of the nucleus.

When the nucleus breaks apart, it releases energy.

Nuclear decay
A nucleus can split and release radiation at any time.

1 lb. (0.45 kg)
of uranium
could power the entire US for nearly 1.5 minutes

Half-life
The time it takes for half of the atoms in a radioactive material to decay

Radiation types

There are three types of radiation. Alpha particles consist of two neutrons and two protons. Beta particles are similar to electrons. Gamma rays are intense bursts of energy. Exposure to very large doses of radiation—as in a nuclear accident or explosion—can be lethal.

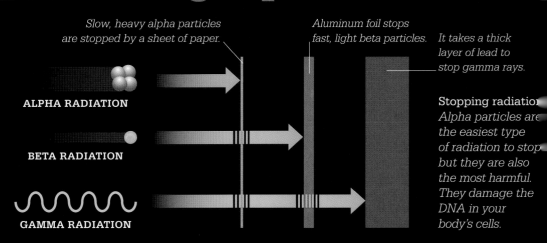

Slow, heavy alpha particles are stopped by a sheet of paper.

Aluminum foil stops fast, light beta particles.

It takes a thick layer of lead to stop gamma rays.

ALPHA RADIATION

BETA RADIATION

GAMMA RADIATION

Stopping radiation Alpha particles are the easiest type of radiation to stop but they are also the most harmful. They damage the DNA in your body's cells.

Energy from atoms

Radioactive uranium is the most energy-rich fuel. Nuclear power stations split uranium nuclei to release energy, which they then use to generate electricity.

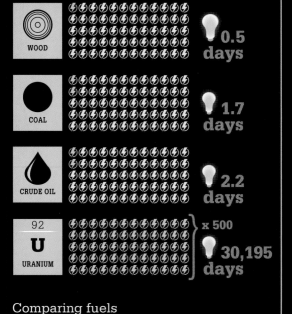

WOOD — 0.5 days

COAL — 1.7 days

CRUDE OIL — 2.2 days

92 **U** URANIUM — x 500 — 30,195 days

Comparing fuels

This chart shows how long 1 lb. (0.45 kg) of different fuels will light a 100-watt bulb.

Background radiation

We are exposed to a small amount of natural radiation every day. This harmless dose is known as background radiation. It comes from space, rocks, soil, plants, food, and animals, as well as from artificial sources.

Food & drink inside your body

Gamma rays from the ground & buildings

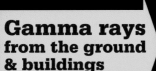

Other sources industrial, nuclear power, weapons tests

Medical scanning & treatment

Cosmic rays from outer space

Radon from granite rocks

Background sources

This diagram shows different sources of background radiation. The wider the arrow, the more radiation we receive from that source.

5,715 years
Carbon-14
(in all living things)

432.2 years
Americium-241
(used in smoke detectors)

3.8 days
Radon-222
(released from rocks)

The number after each element is the sum of protons and neutrons in its nuclei.

24,110 years
Plutonium-239
(used in nuclear fuel and weapons)

1,600 years
Radium-226
(discovered by Marie Curie)

8 days
Iodine-131
(hazardous nuclear waste)

2.7 billion trillionths of a second
Beryllium-13
(created in stars)

Marie Curie

Polish-born Marie Curie (1867–1934) was a real superstar of science. In addition to discovering the radioactive elements polonium and radium, she won Nobel Prizes in physics (1903) and chemistry (1913)—the only person to win in multiple sciences. Curie died from leukemia at the age of 66, probably due to prolonged exposure to radioactive substances. The element curium (96 on the periodic table) is named after her.

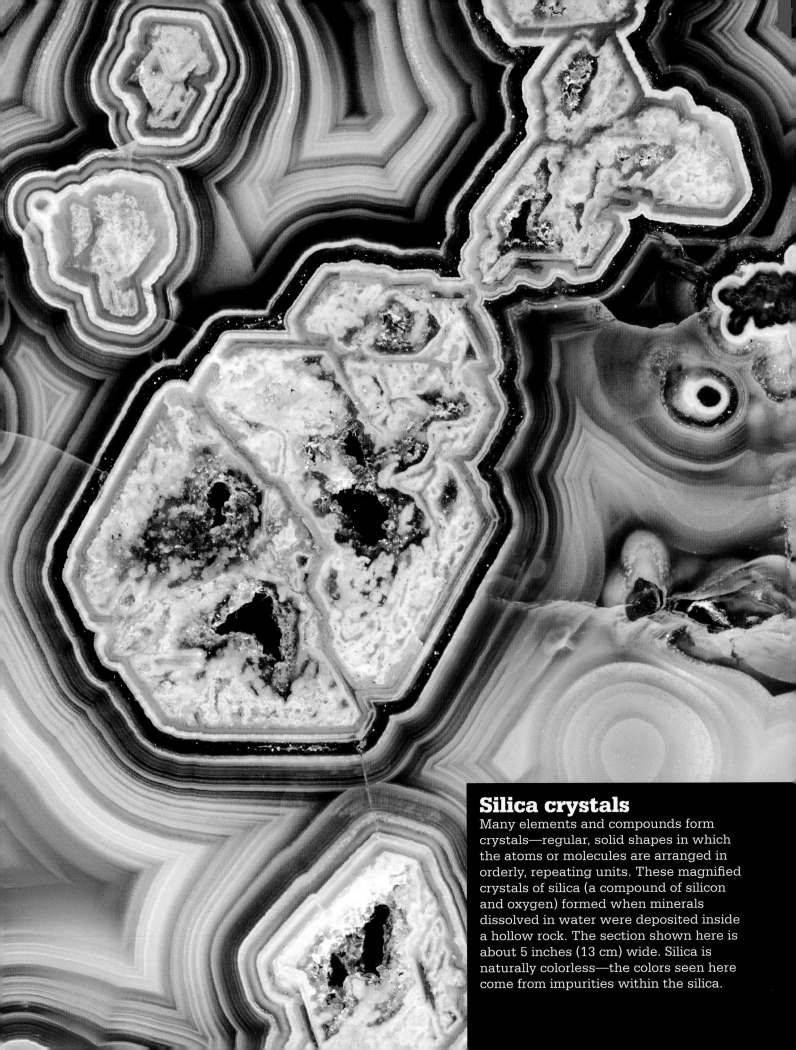

Silica crystals

Many elements and compounds form crystals—regular, solid shapes in which the atoms or molecules are arranged in orderly, repeating units. These magnified crystals of silica (a compound of silicon and oxygen) formed when minerals dissolved in water were deposited inside a hollow rock. The section shown here is about 5 inches (13 cm) wide. Silica is naturally colorless—the colors seen here come from impurities within the silica.

Metalloids [The changelings]

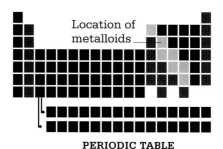

Location of metalloids

PERIODIC TABLE

A thin, diagonal line of metalloids runs across the right of the periodic table. As if undecided about what they want to be, these elements have properties of both metals and nonmetals. Most metalloids can occur in different forms, known as allotropes.

Allotropes

In metalloids and some other elements, the atoms can link up in more than one way to produce allotropes. These are different forms of the same element that look and behave differently.

HARD ARSENIC

Hard or soft?
Arsenic occurs as both a brittle gray allotrope and a soft yellow one.

SOFT ARSENIC

Boron

| 5 |
| B |
| BORON |

Versatile boron is used in laundry bleaches and soaps and as a cockroach killer. Added to glass, it gives greater resistance to temperature changes. Added to steel, it gives extra hardness.

What it is	A brown powder; black crystals
Melting point	3,769°F (2,076°C)
Boiling point	7,101°F (3,927°C)

The long haul
Mule trains once hauled wagons of boron ore from US mines. This train marked the opening of a new mine in 1957.

Germanium

| 32 |
| Ge |
| GERMANIUM |

Combined with silicon as a metal alloy, this element forms an ideal semiconductor (see opposite page) for high-speed electronic circuits. Germanium is also used to make lenses.

What it is	A brittle, silvery-white metalloid
Melting point	1,720.9°F (938.3°C)
Boiling point	5,108°F (2,820°C)

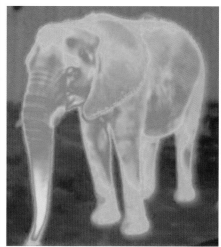

Glowing giant
Infrared cameras, which detect heat, use germanium in their lenses.

Antimony

| 51 |
| Sb |
| ANTIMONY |

Known for thousands of years, antimony was used by the ancient Egyptians in black eye shadow and mascara. Today it is added as a hardener to metal alloys, and it is an ingredient in many flame-resistant materials.

What it is	A bright silvery metal; brittle black crystals; yellow crystals
Melting point	1,167.13°F (630.63°C)
Boiling point	2,889°F (1,587°C)

Arsenic

| 33 |
| As |
| ARSENIC |

This element is toxic to nearly all life, apart from some tough types of bacteria. It was once a favorite poison of murderers, because its presence in a dead body was difficult to detect.

Potent poison
When taken into the body, arsenic causes organ failure.

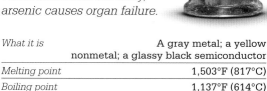

What it is	A gray metal; a yellow nonmetal; a glassy black semiconductor
Melting point	1,503°F (817°C)
Boiling point	1,137°F (614°C)

Other metalloids:
Tellurium (Te); Polonium (Po)

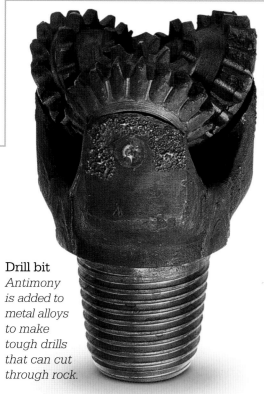

Drill bit
Antimony is added to metal alloys to make tough drills that can cut through rock.

Amethyst
These purple amethyst crystals are made of the compound silicon dioxide (silicon and oxygen). Tiny amounts of impurities give the crystals their color.

14
Si
SILICON

Silicon

A major ingredient of Earth's crust, silicon is important in the manufacture of glass, ceramics, and concrete. But this metalloid is best known as a semiconductor. A semiconductor does not conduct electricity as well as a metal does, but the current it transmits can be controlled. There are tiny silicon switches in every electronic device.

What it is	A shiny gray metalloid
Melting point	2,577°F (1,414°C)
Boiling point	5,252°F (2,900°C)
Special features	Semiconductor silicon: purest substance ever made

Nonm
ga

* Why do explosives go bang?

* What do elements do inside your body?

* Which element protects race-car drivers from fire?

etals &
ses

Nonmetals & gases

The last few groups of the periodic table are filled with nonmetals, many of which are gases. Here you will find elements essential to life—including carbon, oxygen, and nitrogen—as well as the furiously reactive halogen gases and the extremely unreactive noble gases.

Mixed bunch

The nonmetals lie on the right of the periodic table. Although they are few in number, the nonmetals are more varied and interesting than many metals. With significantly lower melting and boiling points than metals (excluding carbon), most of these elements are gases. They are also poor conductors of heat and electricity.

WARNING! DON'T TRY THIS AT HOME

Phosphorus and oxygen

These photographs show the reaction between nonmetals phosphorus (Group 15) and oxygen (Group 16). The experiment was performed under strict laboratory conditions.

14	15	16	17	18
				2 **He** HELIUM
6 **C** CARBON	7 **N** NITROGEN	8 **O** OXYGEN	9 **F** FLUORINE	10 **Ne** NEON
	15 **P** PHOSPHORUS	16 **S** SULFUR	17 **Cl** CHLORINE	18 **Ar** ARGON
		34 **Se** SELENIUM	35 **Br** BROMINE	36 **Kr** KRYPTON
			53 **I** IODINE	54 **Xe** XENON
			85 **At** ASTATINE	86 **Rn** RADON

Noble gases (beige)

Nonmetals (shown in blue)

Halogens (orange)

1 A round flask is filled with pure oxygen gas. Then a small lump of the nonmetal phosphorus is placed on the sand in the bottom.

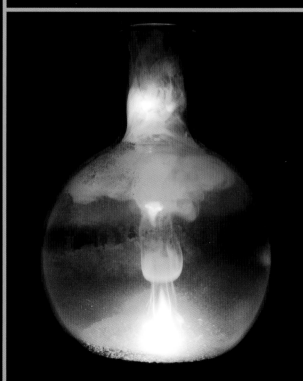

2 The lump of phosphorus reacts with the oxygen in the flask. The phosphorus first begins to smoke, and soon it ignites.

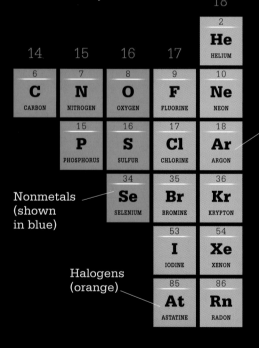

There is enough phosphorus in the human body to make 200 matches

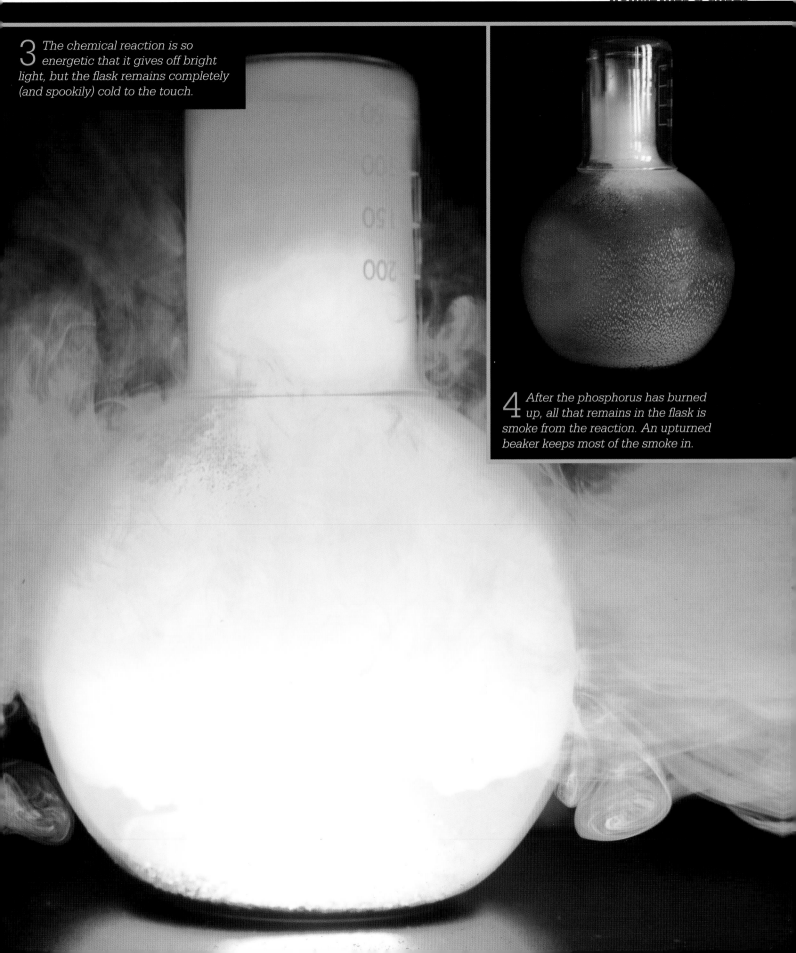

3 The chemical reaction is so energetic that it gives off bright light, but the flask remains completely (and spookily) cold to the touch.

4 After the phosphorus has burned up, all that remains in the flask is smoke from the reaction. An upturned beaker keeps most of the smoke in.

Many elements are vital for life, but those that have no role in the body can be lethal once inside it. It may be a single element that wreaks havoc, or a combination of elements—such as cyanide (a substance made of carbon and nitrogen)—that does the harm.

Murder in mind

The Borgias were a ruthless family in Italy whose enemies did not last long. Lucrezia Borgia is said to have worn a hollow ring in which she kept a poison made of arsenic, phosphorus, and copper.

LUCREZIA BORGIA (1480–1519)

Know your poison

When unwanted elements enter our bodies, they damage organs and change the behavior of cells. But people did not always know about their deadly properties, and some famous folks suffered at the hands of these toxic terrors.

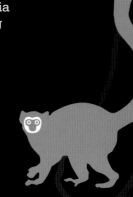

The bamboo **lemur** consumes **enough cyanide** daily to kill a human

Dead from lead?

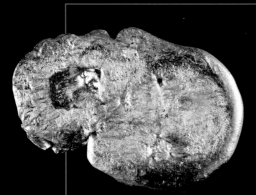

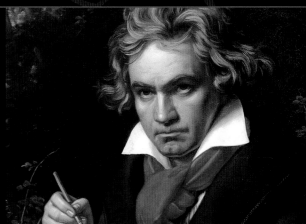

Scientists disagree about what caused the death of the composer Ludwig van Beethoven, but it could have been lead. He took lead-laced medicines for his ailments, and we now know that even a tiny amount of lead can damage the body.

LUDWIG VAN BEETHOVEN (1770–1827)

Mind-bending mercury

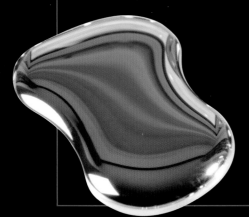

Abraham Lincoln, the 16th president, treated his fits of rage and depression with "little blue pills," whose main ingredient was toxic mercury. He was shot in 1865—but if the bullet hadn't killed him, the mercury eventually would have!

ABRAHAM LINCOLN (1809–1865)

Awful arsenic

Impressionist artists of the 19th century went mad for Paris green—literally! This vivid green paint contained arsenic. Paul Cézanne's diabetes, Vincent van Gogh's mental problems, and Claude Monet's blindness were likely caused by this toxic paint.

CLAUDE MONET (1840–1926)

Radioactive radium

Radium kills by releasing lethal radiation into the body. Marie Curie (far right), the discoverer of radium, carried radioactive material around in her pocket, unaware of the dangers. She eventually died of radiation sickness.

MARIE CURIE (1867–1934)

Polonium peril

Not all deaths from toxic elements are accidental. The Russian ex-spy Alexander Litvinenko was murdered in London in 2006. His food was poisoned with polonium, a radioactive element, and he died three weeks later.

ALEXANDER LITVINENKO (1962–2006)

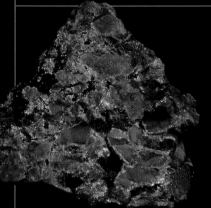

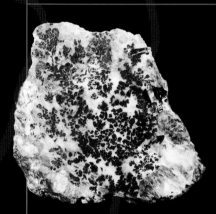

World War I military cemetery, Belgium
Chlorine was used as poison gas in World War I, carried by the wind over enemy positions. When the wind changed, it often blew the gas over the attackers instead.

91,000
soldiers died from poison gas attacks during World War I

Oxygen [The spark of life]

8
O
OXYGEN

As a component of water, oxygen covers most of the planet's surface and is vital for life. And as a gas that makes up 21 percent of the air that you breathe, oxygen drives chemical processes in your body. This reactive element is also at the heart of every fire that burns.

Oxygen (O₂)
An oxygen gas molecule is made up of two linked oxygen atoms.

Element profile

Name	Oxygen
Symbol	O
Atomic number	8
What it is	A colorless, odorless gas
Melting point	−360.9°F (−218.3°C)
Boiling point	−297.2°F (−182.9°C)
Special features	Most common element in Earth's crust; essential for life; light blue as a liquid

Giant dragonfly fossil
Around 300 million years ago, atmospheric oxygen reached a peak of 35 percent, allowing insects, such as Meganeura, to grow to giant sizes.

Ancient air

The atmosphere of the young Earth would have been deadly to us, since it contained no oxygen. Gradually, oxygen began to build up in the air as it was released by ocean life-forms called blue-green algae.

Meganeura's wingspan was over 2.5 feet (75 cm).

Oxygen
in the atmosphere began building up
2.5 billion
years ago

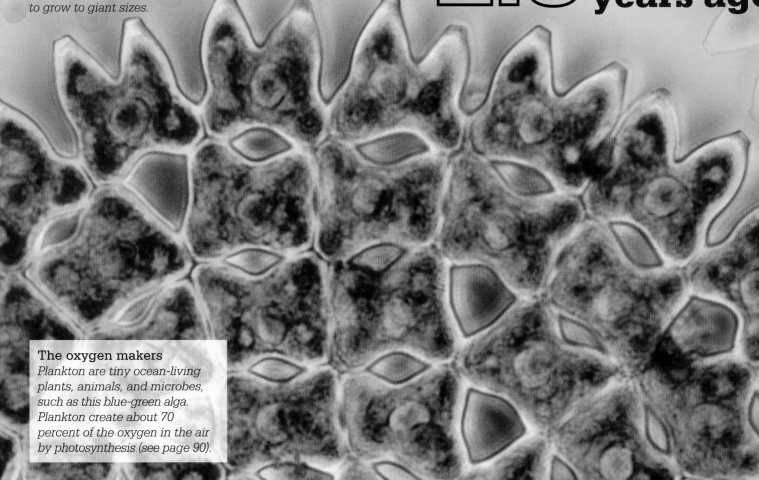

The oxygen makers
Plankton are tiny ocean-living plants, animals, and microbes, such as this blue-green alga. Plankton create about 70 percent of the oxygen in the air by photosynthesis (see page 90).

The great reactor

Oxygen is very reactive. Burning, for example, is a reaction between a substance, such as wood, and oxygen in the air. Because of oxygen's reactivity, most of Earth's oxygen is locked up in the crust, bound to other elements as oxide compounds.

Wildfire
When there is an abundant supply of oxygen and plenty of material to burn, it's difficult to stop a fire.

Making oxygen

The oxygen needed for industrial processes such as steelmaking (see page 58) is obtained from air by a process known as distillation. This "manufactured" oxygen is also used in hospitals and aircraft.

Lifesaving gas
Manufactured oxygen allows astronauts, mountain climbers, and divers to breathe in extreme and dangerous environments.

Wrapped in gas

Earth's atmosphere is mostly oxygen and nitrogen, with small amounts of other gases. There are layers within the atmosphere, each with a different temperature and a slightly different mix of gases. The ozone layer is rich in a form of oxygen called ozone.

OZONE MOLECULE

Ozone (O₃)
An ozone molecule consists of three oxygen atoms. The ozone layer protects living things from the Sun's harmful ultraviolet (UV) rays.

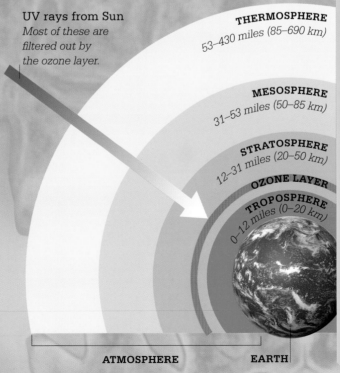

UV rays from Sun
Most of these are filtered out by the ozone layer.

THERMOSPHERE
53–430 miles (85–690 km)

MESOSPHERE
31–53 miles (50–85 km)

STRATOSPHERE
12–31 miles (20–50 km)

OZONE LAYER

TROPOSPHERE
0–12 miles (0–20 km)

ATMOSPHERE   EARTH

More here

ozone layer forest fire cyanobacteria **plankton stromatolite** respiration combustion **death zone water** liquid oxygen atmosphere **ultraviolet distillation** *Meganeura*

Get experimenting!
To see how burning relies on oxygen, ask an adult to place an upturned glass jar over a lighted candle. The flame will go out, but only after it has used up all the oxygen in the jar.

burning: a chemical reaction in which a substance combines with oxygen, releasing heat.

distillation: the process of heating a liquid mixture to separate out its components. To distill air, the air has to first be cooled so that it turns into a liquid.

photosynthesis: the process by which plants use the energy in sunlight to make food from carbon dioxide and water. Oxygen is released as a waste product (see pages 90–91).

Elements in sports

In track cycling, good equipment is crucial—anything that shaves a second off your time can make you a winner! Bikes have lightweight carbon-fiber frames molded into streamlined shapes. Strong aluminum alloy is used for the wheels. The hard carbon-fiber shell of the padded helmet gives vital protection when you're pedaling at 53 miles per hour (85 kph), with no brakes, and another cyclist is just inches behind you!

Carbon [It's got the power!]

6		
C		
CARBON		

The vast majority of known compounds contain carbon. This element is so good at forming compounds because each carbon atom can link with up to four other atoms. Carbon compounds are the basis of life, and they provide us with fuels and other useful materials.

Element profile

Name	Carbon
Symbol	C
Atomic number	6
What it is	A black or clear nonmetal solid
Melting point	6,400°F (3,500°C)
Boiling point	7,281°F (4,027°C)
Special features	Forms big molecules that are essential to living things

Natural carbon

Carbon can occur naturally in different forms, known as allotropes (see page 72). Sparkling diamond, which is the hardest of all natural substances, is pure carbon. So, too, is the soft graphite used for pencil "lead."

DIAMOND   **GRAPHITE**

The energizers

Carbohydrates, such as sugars and starches, are compounds of carbon, hydrogen, and oxygen. Carbohydrates supply animals and plants with energy to fuel their body processes.

Carbon-based life

Most of your body tissues are made up of carbon-containing proteins, carbohydrates, and fats. Carbon also forms the backbone of the DNA molecule (see page 80) found in all your cells.

Living carbon
Almost every part of your body contains the element carbon.

Carbohydrates in food
Starchy foods, such as cereals, bread, potatoes, rice, beans, and pasta, are packed with energy-giving carbohydrates.

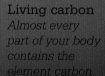

Fossil fuels

Coal, crude oil, and natural gas are called fossil fuels. This is because they are formed from the fossilized, carbon-rich remains of long-dead plants and animals. When we burn these fuels, they release lots of energy, which we can use to generate electricity, power industry, and fuel our cars.

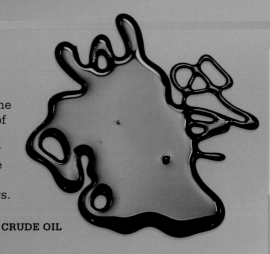

CRUDE OIL

80% of the energy we use comes from burning fossil fuels

Environmental impact

Burning fossil fuels produces polluting gases that are dangerous to our health and to the environment. They also absorb heat and warm the planet. This "global warming" is threatening to upset the balance of life on Earth (see page 91).

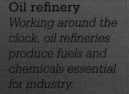

Oil refinery
Working around the clock, oil refineries produce fuels and chemicals essential for industry.

Products from oil

Crude oil is a liquid mix of hydrocarbons (hydrogen-carbon compounds). Refineries heat oil until it turns to gas. As the gas cools, the different hydrocarbons in the mixture condense back to liquids at different temperatures.

COOL　　　SUBSTANCE

Liquid petroleum gas, below 68°F (20°C)
Used for cooking and for making plastics.

Gasoline, 70°F–160°F (20°C–70°C)
An explosive fuel used in car engines.

Naphtha, 160°F–320°F (70°C–160°C)
A yellow liquid used for making chemicals.

Kerosene, 320°F–480°F (160°C–250°C)
A light, oily liquid used for jet fuel.

Diesel, 480°F–660°F (250°C–350°C)
Liquid fuel used in some truck engines.

Fuel oil, 660°F–715°F (350°C–380°C)
Heavy fuel for ships and power stations.

Lubricating oil and bitumen, over 715°F (380°C)
Grease, lubricants, and tar for road building and roofing.

HOT

Carbon for life [The key cycle]

Combined with oxygen as the gas carbon dioxide
(CO_2), carbon is present in Earth's atmosphere.
Plants need this CO_2 to make their food. All animals
eat either plants or other animals. So without CO_2,
there would be no life on Earth.

Sucking up carbon

Plants get the carbon they need to
build their "bodies" directly from the air.
Using energy from the Sun, they turn
CO_2 and water into glucose
(a simple sugar molecule)
by a process called
photosynthesis.

WATER FROM
ROOTS

Leafy business
*Photosynthesis takes place
inside the leaves of plants.
It uses water taken up
by the roots and CO_2
absorbed from the air.*

SUNLIGHT

Surface cells

Chloroplasts
*The Sun's energy
is captured by tiny
structures in the plant
cell called chloroplasts.*

Sugar-making cells

Leaf pores
*Holes on the underside
allow CO_2 to enter
the leaf and oxygen
(a waste product
of photosynthesis)
to escape.*

CARBON
DIOXIDE
IN

OXYGEN
OUT

Building with sugar
*The glucose sugar made
in the leaves provides
food for the plant. It is
also converted into a
substance called
cellulose, which is used
to build plant cells.*

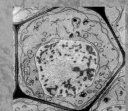

PLANT CELL

Greenhouse effect

Carbon dioxide and other gases in the atmosphere warm Earth by trapping the Sun's heat, just like a greenhouse does. Without these gases, Earth would be a freezing −0.4°F (−18°C) and too cold for life.

EARTH FROM SPACE

The carbon cycle

Carbon, in the form of CO_2, circulates naturally between the atmosphere, living things, and the land and oceans.

CO_2 in the atmosphere

Photosynthesis

Green plants absorb CO_2.

Animals eat plants and breathe out CO_2.

Oceans absorb and release CO_2.

Plants and animals die and their remains are incorporated into the ground.

Plant and animal remains form fossil fuels.

Too much CO₂

When a fossil fuel (see page 89) burns, carbon locked up in the fuel combines with oxygen to form CO_2, which escapes into the air. We are adding so much extra CO_2 into the atmosphere that Earth is overheating.

6		8		8
C	+	**O**		**O**
CARBON		OXYGEN		OXYGEN

$$= CO_2$$

Boiled egg: 11.5 oz. (330 g) of CO_2

Glass of orange juice: 8 oz. (225 g) of CO_2

Cereal and milk: 2.6 lbs. (1.2 kg) of CO_2

Slice of toast: 2 oz. (60 g) of CO_2

Carbon footprint

Every time we use fossil fuels, an amount of CO_2 is released—a "carbon footprint" is left behind. The footprint left by producing the food in this breakfast is 3.9 lbs. (1.8 kg) of CO_2.

Capturing carbon

Rain forests, such as this one in Borneo, collect huge amounts of carbon as they absorb CO_2. They also release a lot of oxygen gas into the atmosphere.

Halogens [Caution required!]

Location of halogens

PERIODIC TABLE

Everything about the halogens is intense. This is a group of colorful, feisty, nonmetallic elements on the right of the periodic table. The halogens react violently with most things, and it takes a lot of energy to break up the compounds that they form.

Iodine

53	
I	
IODINE	

Make sure you eat your greens—they contain lots of iodine, which helps your body develop healthily. Iodine is also a great antiseptic, used to keep wounds free from infection.

Evaporating iodine
When heated, iodine quickly evaporates to form a beautiful purple gas.

What it is	A purplish-black solid
Melting point	236.66°F (113.7°C)
Boiling point	363.7°F (184.3°C)

Bromine

35	
Br	
BROMINE	

Brown bromine stinks—its name comes from the Greek for "stench of goats"! Known since ancient times, it was an ingredient of the purple dye worn by the rulers of Rome. Bromine occurs in large quantities in the Dead Sea.

Liquid brown
Although liquid at room temperature, bromine is always on the point of turning into a foul-smelling gas.

Flame fighter
Bromine compounds are great at resisting flames, so they are used in fireproof materials.

RACE-CAR DRIVER IN FIREPROOF SUIT

What it is	A smoking red-brown liquid
Melting point	19°F (−7.3°C)
Boiling point	138°F (59°C)

Chlorine

17	
Cl	
CHLORINE	

Chlorine can be lethal to living things. But tiny amounts of chlorine are added to drinking water to kill germs. It has saved millions of people from dying of waterborne diseases such as cholera and typhoid.

What it is	A pale green gas
Melting point	−150.7°F (−101.5°C)
Boiling point	−29.27°F (−34.04°C)

Swimming smell
Chlorine kills germs in pools, but its smell lingers in the water.

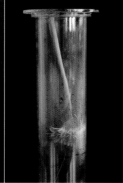

The color thief
In the presence of water, chlorine makes short work of bright colors.

1 *A wet, bright red flower is placed into a jar of chlorine gas. There is a rapid reaction.*

2 *The chlorine bleaches the color from the flower, turning it almost white.*

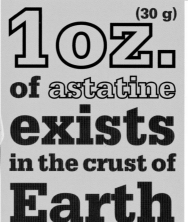

1 oz. (30 g)
of astatine
exists
in the crust of
Earth

Astatine

85	
At	
ASTATINE	

One of the world's rarest elements, astatine forms only from the radioactive decay (see pages 64–65) of other elements. Astatine quickly decays after it forms—then it's gone again! It was first made artificially in 1947.

What it is	A radioactive black solid
Melting point	576°F (302°C)
Boiling point	639°F (337°C)

Fluorite crystals
Halogens react violently with metals to form stable compounds called salts. These crystals of fluorite are an example of a salt formed by fluorine with calcium.

9
F
FLUORINE

Fluorine

Fluorine gas readily bursts into flame, and it attacks any vessel it is kept in. Because of this, it can form stable (unreactive) compounds. Fluorine compounds are put in toothpaste to protect teeth. They also form nonstick coatings for skis and cooking pans.

What it is	A yellow-green gas
Melting point	−363.32°F (−219.62°C)
Boiling point	−306.62°F (−188.12°C)
Special features	The most reactive element in the Universe

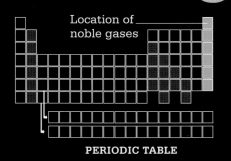

Location of noble gases

PERIODIC TABLE

These "shy" gases, which make up about 1 percent of Earth's atmosphere, rarely combine with other elements. They are all colorless and odorless, but when given a chance to shine they can be dazzling!

Neon

10 Ne NEON

Like all noble gases, neon glows when electricity passes through it. Neon lights blaze bright red-orange, bringing glamour and glitz to city nightlife.

What it is	A colorless, unreactive gas
Melting point	−415.46°F (−248.59°C)
Boiling point	−410.94°F (−246.08°C)

City lights
The first neon lights were made in the 1900s. They changed the look of cities forever.

Radon

86 Rn RADON

This noble gas is radioactive. Radon gas is produced by the radioactive decay (see pages 64–65) of uranium in Earth's crust, and it seeps naturally out of the ground.

What it is	A radioactive gas
Melting point	−96°F (−71°C)
Boiling point	−79.1°F (−61.7°C)

HeNeArKrXe

| HELIUM GAS GLOWING | NEON GAS GLOWING | ARGON GAS GLOWING | KRYPTON GAS GLOWING | XENON GAS GLOWING |

Argon

18 Ar ARGON

Unreactive argon is used in traditional lightbulbs, which heat a filament—a coil of tungsten wire—until it glows. The argon keeps the filament from burning out.

What it is	Unreactive gas
Melting point	−308.7°F (−189.3°C)
Boiling point	−302.4°F (−185.8°C)

Xenon

54 Xe XENON

This gas glows pale violet under electric current. Xenon is used in the superbright, high-temperature headlights of many expensive cars.

Dazzle danger
Headlights that use xenon give excellent night visibility, but they can dazzle other road users.

What it is	An unreactive, heavy gas
Melting point	−169.1°F (−111.7°C)
Boiling point	−162°F (−108°C)

Krypton

36 Kr KRYPTON

Under electric current, krypton glows a whitish-mauve color. Krypton is the main gas used in low-energy fluorescent lights.

Energy saver
Low-energy fluorescent lights use five times less energy than traditional filament lightbulbs.

What it is	An unreactive, heavier-than-air gas
Melting point	−251.25°F (−157.36°C)
Boiling point	−243.8°F (−153.22°C)

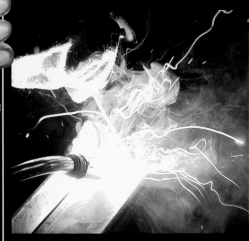

Welding metals together
Argon is so unreactive that it is used to prevent explosions from taking place during dangerous work, such as welding.

6 very unreactive elements

24%
of the mass of elements in our galaxy is
helium

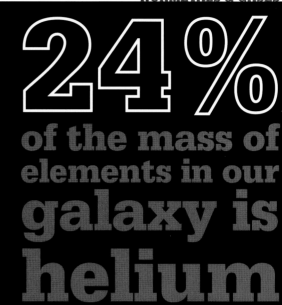

Pure purple power
The color of glowing helium varies from pale peach (see opposite page) to purple, depending on the purity of the gas. This is a very pure sample.

2	
He	
HELIUM	

Helium

This lighter-than-air element is used as a lifting gas in balloons and airships. It is safer than hydrogen (see pages 34–35) because it is nonflammable. Helium has the lowest boiling point of any element, and it is used in liquid form to cool nuclear reactors.

What it is	A lighter-than-air gas
Melting point	−458°F (−272.2°C)
Boiling point	−452.07°F (−268.93°C)
Special features	The second most common element in the Universe

Recycling elements

Earth has a limited supply of elements, and most are locked up inside minerals in its rocky crust. Extracting elements from their minerals requires energy, so it makes sense to recycle them rather than produce fresh material. For example, recycling just one aluminum can save enough energy to run a TV for three hours.

Many elements can be recovered from old electronics. The tracks of circuit boards are copper, while gold and silver are often used for circuit connectors. Computer screens contain silicon and lead, and silicon is also in microchips. Laptop batteries contain lithium, or nickel and cadmium, plus mercury. Tin, lead, iron, aluminum, and titanium are also in electronic devices.

Histo
disco

* Who first described elements?

* Where was the largest gold nugget found?

* Which early space vehicle was made with titanium?

ry of

very

Element quest [Getting to

From the earliest civilizations right up until the present time, the world's greatest minds have struggled with two basic questions: What are the simplest and purest parts of matter? And how many of them are there?

Air
Hot and wet element

Fire
Hot and dry element

Earth
Cold and dry element

Water
Cold and wet element

28,000–22,000 BCE
Cave painting
During the Stone Age, colorful manganese compounds are used to make cave paintings.

450 BCE
Greek elements
Philosophers in ancient Greece believe that just four simple substances combine to make everything: earth, fire, air, and water.

360 BCE
The word element is used for the first time by Plato, the Greek philosopher.

1–300 CE
Lead pipes bring water to Roman towns. The Romans do not realize that lead is toxic.

904 CE
Armies in China use gunpowder made of potassium nitrate and sulfur in their "flying fire" arrows.

• **1000** BCE • • • • • **900** CE • • **1200** CE • **1300**

3300 BCE
The Bronze Age begins when copper extracted from rocks is mixed with tin.

1300 BCE
The Iron Age starts as people learn how to extract iron from its rocky ore.

900–350 BCE
Manganese in the iron ore used by the Spartans makes their weapons superior.

14th century
Glassworks
The glassmakers of Venice begin to use compounds of copper, cobalt, and manganese to add colors to their beautiful glass.

VENETIAN GLASS

ca. 721–ca. 815 CE
Jãbir ibn Hayyãn
The Arabian alchemist (early chemist) Jãbir ibn Hayyãn finds that some substances can be broken down into simpler components, but others, such as gold and silver, always stay the same.

JÃBIR IBN HAYYÃN WITH HIS ALCHEMY EQUIPMENT

1280
Philosopher's stone
Albertus Magnus, a friar, is rumored to have discovered a substance that can change ordinary metals into gold.

GOLD NUGGET

1774
Priestley vs. Lavoisier

Scientific showdown! French chemist Antoine Lavoisier uses English scientist Joseph Priestley's methods and claims to have found a new element. Priestley gets the credit, but Lavoisier gets to name the element oxygen.

JOSEPH PRIESTLEY
English champion

Invented: soda water
Discovered: 6 gases; 1 element

ANTOINE LAVOISIER
French champion

Invented: a new scientific basis for chemistry

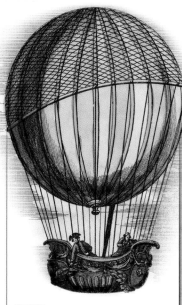

1783
First flight
In France, the first piloted flight of a hydrogen-filled balloon takes place.

1425
Barsbay, the Mamluk sultan of Egypt, circulates a pure gold coin known as an ashrafi.

1714
The mercury thermometer is invented by German physicist Daniel Gabriel Fahrenheit.

1772
Carl Scheele discovers oxygen, but his findings are published only after Joseph Priestley discovers it independently in 1774.

●**1400** ● ● ●**1500** ● **1600 ●** ● ● ●**1700●** ● ● ● ● ● ●

1669
German alchemist Hennig Brand obtains phosphorus by boiling 50 buckets of urine!

1766
English chemist Henry Cavendish discovers hydrogen, which he calls "inflammable air."

1789
Antoine Lavoisier compiles a list of elements. It includes hydrogen, zinc, oxygen, nitrogen, phosphorus, mercury, and sulfur.

1436
Printing press
In Germany, Johannes Gutenberg builds a printing press that uses movable type. The type is made of a lead, tin, and antimony alloy. Suddenly it is much easier to spread scientific ideas.

REPLICA OF GUTENBERG'S PRINTING PRESS

1800
Volta's battery
Alessandro Volta, an Italian nobleman, invents the first battery. It provides a new way of splitting up compounds using electricity.

Copper disc

Paper disc soaked in salt water

Zinc disc

VOLTA'S BATTERY

New ideas [Technology

HUMPHRY DAVY

English champion

Invented: miner's safety light

Discovered: 6 elements

1807
Electro-chemistry

Humphry Davy uses Volta's battery (see page 101) to split up substances with electricity. In this way, Davy discovers the elements sodium and potassium.

1869
Largest gold nugget

"Welcome Stranger," the largest single gold nugget ever found, is excavated from the ground at Moliagul, in Victoria, Australia.

154 lbs.
(70 kg): the weight
of gold
extracted from
Welcome Stranger
after smelting

1879
Light bringer

American inventor Thomas Edison introduces his filament lamps. The filaments are bamboo threads that have been heated until they turn into carbon.

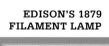

EDISON'S 1879 FILAMENT LAMP

1805
English schoolteacher John Dalton figures out the link between elements and atoms.

1849
The gold rush at Sutter's Mill, California, attracts 300,000 prospectors thirsty for riches.

•1800   **1825•**   **•1850**   **1875•**

1810
In the UK, Peter Durand patents the tin can, made with tinplate steel and sealed with toxic lead.

1828
Swedish chemist Jöns Jakob Berzelius (discoverer of six elements) introduces letters to symbolize elements.

1844
Charles Goodyear, an American inventor, strengthens rubber with sulfur, enabling more durable tires and shoe soles to be made.

1876
Copper wires used to connect telephones allow the first long-distance calls to be made.

1869
Periodic table

Dmitri Mendeleev, a Russian chemist, produces his first periodic table. Other chemists have identified families of elements but cannot make the 63 known elements fit a pattern. Mendeleev's genius is to leave gaps in his table for undiscovered elements.

MENDELEEV'S FIRST PERIODIC TABLE

23 in.
(58.4 cm): the largest
bubble gum
bubble ever blown

1888
Chrome yellow

The Dutch artist Vincent van Gogh paints his vibrant Sunflowers series of pictures. The intensity of the colors is made possible by new artificial pigments such as chrome yellow, which is made with the element chromium (see page 57).

SUNFLOWERS, VINCENT VAN GOGH, 1888

1906
Bubble gum

The first bubble gum, Blibber-Blubber, has sulfur in its recipe. It is not successful—it bursts into a sticky mess when blown. Dubble Bubble gum solves the problem in 1928 by including stretchy latex in its ingredients.

GUM BALLS

1898

Scottish chemist William Ramsey discovers the noble gases krypton, neon, and argon.

1932

English physicist James Chadwick bombards beryllium with radiation and discovers the neutron.

1900   **1925**

1886

Coca-Cola is invented by Dr. John Pemberton, an Atlanta pharmacist. The drink contains phosphoric acid, a compound of phosphorus.

1900

Waterproof cellophane film is invented by treating plant material with sodium sulfate.

1909–1913

German chemists Fritz Haber and Carl Bosch develop a process to make ammonia by reacting nitrogen with hydrogen.

1912

Physicists Ernest Rutherford and Niels Bohr come up with a new theory of the atom.

MARIE CURIE

Polish champion

Invented: theory of radioactivity

Discovered: 2 elements

1898
Radioactivity

Polish-born chemist Marie Curie (see pages 66–67) discovers radioactive polonium and radium with her husband, Pierre, a French scientist, in Paris. She develops a theory of radioactivity that changes the way we think about atoms.

1903
First powered flight

To reduce the weight of their plane, the *Flyer*, the Wright brothers cast its engine block from aluminum. The usual cast-iron block would have been too heavy for takeoff.

THE WRIGHTS' FLYER

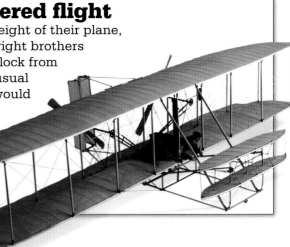

Creating elements [Adding

1945
Atom bomb
During World War II, the US develops atomic bombs. The first bomb, made using uranium, is dropped on Hiroshima, Japan, on August 6. Three days later, a second bomb, which uses plutonium, strikes the city of Nagasaki.

ATOMIC BOMB
BLAST

1957
Sputnik I
The first vehicle into space, the satellite *Sputnik I*, is launched by the USSR. It is protected by a heat-resistant shield of aluminum-magnesium-titanium alloy. The shield is just 0.04 inch (1 mm) thick, yet very tough.

SPUTNIK I
SATELLITE

1935
Synthetic nylon, designed to replace silk, is produced by American chemist Wallace Carothers.

1938
Teflon (PTFE)—a carbon and fluorine compound—is developed. It is used to make nonstick coatings, bearings, sealants, fabrics, and more.

1952
Einsteinium and fermium are discovered in the debris of the nuclear test of the first hydrogen atomic bomb, "Ivy Mike."

1955
The first superaccurate atomic clock, regulated by cesium atoms, goes on sale.

1935 ● **1945** ● **1955** ●

1937
The Hindenburg—*the last great hydrogen-filled airship—explodes, killing 35 people (see pages 34–35).*

1949
American Willard Libby invents a way of dating ancient objects using radioactive carbon-14.

1959
The popular plastic doll Barbie goes on sale.

GLENN T. SEABORG
American champion

Invented: the actinide series

Discovered: 10 elements

1951
New elements
While working at the University of California, Berkeley, American chemist Glenn T. Seaborg identifies several new elements that are heavier than uranium. These unstable elements are made in particle accelerators.

1960
Laser
American physicist Theodore Maiman invents the laser, which makes intense light beams. The color of the light depends on which elements are used in the laser. Argon, for example, gives blue.

LASER LIGHT SHOW

1981
Space shuttle

The space shuttle *Columbia*, the first-ever reusable space vehicle, makes its first flight. The craft is built from aluminum alloy, with titanium alloy used for the engine housing. The space shuttle's detachable boosters are encased in steel.

SPACE SHUTTLE READY FOR ITS FIRST LAUNCH

2004
Diamond in the sky

The Universe's biggest known diamond is detected in the core of a white dwarf star in the constellation Centaurus. This lump of crystallized carbon is 1,865 miles (3,000 km) wide and weighs about 2.5 thousand trillion trillion tons.

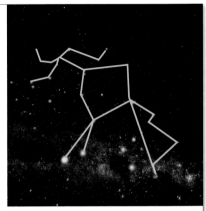

THE CONSTELLATION CENTAURUS

By comparison, the **largest uncut diamond ever found on Earth weighed 22 OZ. (621 g)**

1966

The synthetic fiber Kevlar, invented by American chemist Stephanie Kwolek, is patented. Five times stronger than steel, it is made of carbon, hydrogen, nitrogen, and oxygen.

•1965 • • •1975 • • •1985 • • •1995 • •2005 • 2015•

1965

American James T. Russell patents the compact disc (CD). It records data on a reflective layer of aluminum.

1967

An artificial nylon turf (a hydrogen-carbon-nitrogen compound) is patented in the United States.

1983

Motorola's DynaTAC 8000X is the first personal, handheld cell phone to go on sale. It has a nickel-vanadium battery.

1999

The world's largest silver and lead mine is established at Cannington, Queensland, Australia.

2011

Elements 114 and 116 are added to the periodic table.

1961
Microchip

In Texas, Jack Kilby makes the first microchip—a slice of germanium carrying tiny linked electronic components. It enables electronic devices to be made much smaller.

MAGNIFIED VIEW OF MICROCHIP SURFACE

1991
Carbon nanotubes

Sumio Iijima, a Japanese physicist, discovers a new form of carbon—tiny tubes 50,000 times thinner than human hairs. These nanotubes are superstrong and have useful electrical properties.

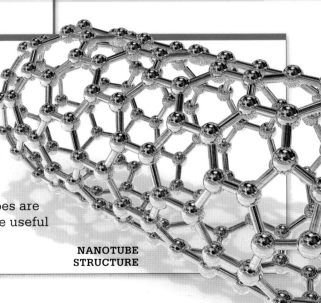

NANOTUBE STRUCTURE

Alkali
A substance that dissolves in water and neutralizes acids; the chemical opposite of an acid. Alkali metals are commonly found combined in alkaline compounds.

Alkaline
Having the properties of an alkali.

Allotrope
One of two or more distinct forms of the same element that have different properties but are the same state of matter (solid, liquid, or gas). Diamond and graphite are solid allotropes of carbon.

Alloy
A metallic mixture made of two or more elements. Alloys include bronze, solder, and steel.

Alpha particle
A particle consisting of two protons and two neutrons that is released when the nucleus of a radioactive atom decays.

Atmosphere
The layer of mixed gases surrounding planet Earth.

Atom
A tiny particle of matter, consisting of protons, neutrons, and electrons. Atoms are the smallest particles that can take part in a chemical reaction.

Atomic bomb
An immensely powerful bomb that releases energy by splitting the nuclei of atoms in a chain reaction.

Atomic clock
A superaccurate clock that uses the natural vibrations of atoms (such as cesium) to count time. Atomic clocks are used to keep the official time standard and to control GPS satellites.

Atomic number
The number of protons in the nucleus of an atom. Elements are arranged on the periodic table in order of increasing atomic number.

Beta particle
A fast-moving electron that is released by the decay of a radioactive nucleus.

Boiling point
The point at which a liquid, when heated, stops increasing in temperature and starts to evaporate, or turn into a gas.

Burning
A type of reaction, between a substance and oxygen in the air, that gives off heat and flames.

Carbohydrate
A chemical compound made up of carbon, hydrogen, and oxygen. Many carbohydrates, including sugar and starch, are vital to life.

Catalyst
A material that helps a chemical reaction take place. The catalyst itself is not used up or changed by the reaction.

Chain reaction
A nuclear reaction that splits the nucleus of an atom, releasing neutrons that then split the nuclei of other atoms. Controlled chain reactions are used in nuclear power stations; uncontrolled chain reactions create nuclear explosions.

Compound
A substance made of two or more elements bonded, or linked, together chemically.

Conductor
A material that allows heat or electricity to pass through it.

Corrosion
The chemical breakdown of the surface of a metal.

Density
A measure of how heavy an object feels. The more weighty the atoms or the more tightly packed they are, the denser the object is.

Distillation
The process of heating a liquid mixture to separate its components. Each component is boiled off at a different temperature, and its gas condenses separately.

DNA
The double spiral–shaped molecule found in the nucleus of every one of the cells in a living body. This special molecule contains all the genetic instructions the body needs to grow and develop. *DNA* stands for *deoxyribonucleic acid*.

Electron
A negatively charged particle that orbits, or moves around, the nucleus of an atom.

Electronic
Relating to electrons. Electronics is the scientific investigation of how electrons move through materials.

Enamel
The tough layer that forms the outer coating of teeth.

Fluorescent
Able to emit light when an electric current passes through a noble gas. Low-energy lightbulbs are fluorescent.

Fossil
The preserved remains or trace of a dead plant or animal.

Fossil fuel
Fuel such as coal, crude oil, or gas, made from the remains of dead plants and animals. When fossil fuels burn, they combine with oxygen and release their stored carbon as carbon dioxide gas.

Fusion
The process that creates a new element by joining the nuclei of atoms.

Gamma ray
A very high-frequency wave of electromagnetic energy released from the nucleus of an atom.

Gas
A state of matter in which the

Element with the highest boiling point: rhenium 10,105°F (5,596°C)

Glossary

atoms are free to move around, enabling the substance to fill any container in which it is placed.

Glucose
The simplest form of sugar. Glucose in food is broken down by the body to release energy.

GPS
A satellite system that involves more than 30 satellites orbiting Earth and tells users their exact location and the correct time. *GPS* stands for *Global Positioning System*.

Half-life
The time it takes for half of the atoms in a sample of a radioactive element to decay.

Hydrocarbon
A compound containing mainly carbon and hydrogen. Most hydrocarbons are found in crude oil.

Impurity
Anything that contaminates or reduces the purity of a substance.

Infrared
Relating to low-frequency waves of electromagnetic energy. Infrared radiation is felt as heat.

Laser
An intense, focused beam of light used for communications, cutting, welding, surgery, astronomy, and much more. *Laser* stands for *Light Amplification by Stimulated Emission of Radiation*.

Liquid
A state of matter between solid and gas. A liquid can flow, and it will always take the shape of its container. Its atoms or molecules settle to form a surface.

Magnet
A substance or object that attracts iron, cobalt, nickel,

Element with the highest melting point: carbon 5,767°F (3,186°C)

and their alloys.

Magnetic
Able to act as a magnet.

Malleable
Able to be bent, shaped, and worked without breaking.

Matter
Any substance that has mass, meaning that it exerts a downward force on Earth. Matter is made up of atoms and can exist in three different states—solid, liquid, or gas.

Melting point
The point at which a solid, when heated, stops increasing in temperature and starts turning into a liquid.

Meteorite
A rock that falls to Earth from space.

Mineral
A naturally occurring solid compound whose atoms are ordered in crystal patterns. Many rocks are made of minerals.

Molecule
A substance made of more than one atom chemically bonded, or linked, together.

Molten
In a liquified state due to heat.

Nebula
A cloud of gas and dust in space.

Neutron
A particle that has no electrical charge, slightly bigger than a proton. There are neutrons in the nuclei of all atoms except those of hydrogen.

Nuclear
Relating to the nucleus, or core, of an atom.

Ore
A rock or mineral that contains a valuable or useful substance.

Osteoblast
A cell that makes new bone.

Particle
A tiny part, such as an atom or molecule, that makes up matter. Atoms themselves are made up of even smaller particles called protons, neutrons, and electrons.

Particle accelerator
A machine that uses magnets to accelerate particles around a track. Collisions between the particles release huge amounts of energy and sometimes create new particles or new elements.

Periodic table
A table of all the elements, arranged in order of increasing atomic number and grouped into "families" of elements that have similar properties.

Photosynthesis
The process by which plants use the energy in sunlight to make food from carbon dioxide and water. Oxygen is released as a waste product of photosynthesis.

Pigment
A substance, often a solid powder, that gives color to paint.

Pollution
The contamination of the environment by harmful substances.

Pressure
The force exerted by a gas on the walls of its container. Air pressure is the force exerted by the atmosphere on Earth's surface.

Property
A characteristic quality of a material or substance.

Proton
A positively charged particle found in the nucleus of an atom.

Radiation
Alpha and beta particles, or intense bursts of energy such as gamma rays, emitted by the nucleus of a radioactive atom.

Radioactive
Emitting nuclear radiation.

Radioactive decay
The natural breakup of atomic nuclei in radioactive elements.

Reaction
A process in which an element or compound combines chemically with another.

Reactive
Likely to react chemically.

Rust
A type of corrosion that happens when iron comes into contact with oxygen and water.

Salt
A compound formed when an acid and an alkali react. Table salt, sodium chloride, is one example.

Semiconductor
A material whose electrical conductivity is between that of a metal and a nonmetal. Semiconductors are often made of metalloid compounds.

Smelting
Extracting metal from its ore by heating the ore in a furnace.

Solid
A state of matter in which the atoms or molecules maintain a rigid shape.

Supernova
A huge explosion that takes place when a star has used up all of its fuel and collapses.

The most expensive elements are synthetic—plutonium can cost 100 times more than gold

Synthetic
Created artificially. Synthetic elements do not occur naturally on Earth. They are made inside nuclear reactors and particle accelerators.

Tissue
A collection of living cells inside the human body. Muscle is an example of body tissue.

Toxic
Harmful to living things.

Unreactive
Unlikely or unable to react chemically.

X-ray
A high-frequency wave of electromagnetic energy released from outside the nucleus of an atom.

GALENA (LEAD ORE)

A

actinium 22, 24, 44, 63, 104
actinoid 22–23, 24–25, 44
air 81, 82
aircraft 30, 34–35, 36, 68, 83, 89, 95, 101, 103, 104
Alexander III, Czar 53
alkali metal 22, 23, 28, 30–31, 41
alkaline earth metal 22, 23, 28, 36–37
allotrope 72, 88
alloy 16, 31, 36, 44, 48, 54, 68, 72, 87, 101, 104, 105
alpha radiation 63, 65
aluminum 23, 25, 41, 44–45, 59, 62, 65, 68, 87, 97, 103, 104, 105
  uses 41, 68, 87
aluminum oxide 68
amalgam 48
americium 22, 25, 44, 63, 65
  uses 63
amethyst 73
antimony 23, 25, 44, 56, 72, 101
  uses 72
antiseptic 92
argon 23, 25, 76, 81, 94, 103, 104
  uses 94
armor 48, 50–51
arsenic 23, 25, 44, 57, 68, 72, 78, 79
  uses 72
astatine 23, 25, 76, 92
astronaut 53
atom 14, 15, 18–19, 21, 28, 30, 32, 64, 65, 71, 72, 81, 102, 103, 104
  chemical bond 81
  electron shell 18

electron 18, 19, 28, 65
neutron 18, 19, 20, 64, 65
nucleus 18, 19, 20, 22, 63, 64
proton 18, 19, 20, 22, 28, 63, 64, 65
theory of 103
atomic bomb 63, 104
  "Ivy Mike" 63, 105
atomic clock 30, 104
atomic number 22, 32
autunite 36

B

Barbie 104
barium 22, 24, 36
  barium meal 36
  uses 36, 41
barium sulfate 36
Barsbay, Sultan 101
Bartholdi, Frédéric 55
battery 17, 30, 97, 101
berkelium 23, 25, 44, 63
beryl 37
beryllium 18, 22, 24, 37, 65, 103
  uses 37
Berzelius, Jöns Jakob 102
beta radiation 65
bismuth 23, 24, 25, 44, 68
  uses 68
bitumen 89
blast furnace 58, 60–61
bleach 72, 92
blue-green algae 82
blueprint 57
Bohr, Niels 103
bohrium 22, 24, 44, 63
bone 38, 56

Borgia, Lucrezia 78
Borgias, the 78
boron 23, 25, 44, 72
  uses 72
Bosch, Carl 103
Brand, Hennig 101
bromine 14, 23, 25, 76, 92
  uses 92
bronze 54, 58
  weapon 54
Bronze Age 54, 100
bubble gum 102, 103
building 39, 58–59
bulletproof material 48
Burj Khalifa 59

C

cadmium 17, 23, 25, 44, 48, 57, 97
cadmium sulfide 57
Caesar, Julius 52
calcium 8, 22, 24, 28, 36, 38–39, 84, 93
  blood 85
  bone 38, 85
  building 39
  muscle 85
  shell 38
  star 39
  tooth 38, 85
calcium phosphate 38, 85
californium 23, 25, 44, 63
car 16–17, 36, 89, 94
carbohydrate 88
carbon 15, 16, 17, 19, 23, 25, 32, 48, 50, 56, 76, 78, 80, 84, 88–91, 104, 105
  allotrope 88
  carbon-14 65, 104
  carbon fiber 87
  coke 58, 61
  diamond 88, 105
  DNA 88
  graphite 88

nanotube 105
  photosynthesis 90
carbon cycle 91
carbon dioxide 19, 90–91
carbon footprint 91
Carothers, Wallace 104
catalytic converter 16, 17, 49
cave painting 56, 100
Cavendish, Henry 101
cell phone 30, 62, 68, 105
cellophane 103
ceramic 17, 73
cerium 22, 24, 44, 62
cesium 22, 24, 28, 30, 104
  uses 30
Cézanne, Paul 79
Chadwick, James 103
charcoal 56, 58
Charles II of England 50
chemical reaction 15, 17, 28–29, 30, 31, 44–45, 76–77, 92
  burning 15, 83
chlorine 15, 16, 23, 25, 76, 79, 92
  uses 92
chromium 22, 24, 25, 31, 37, 44, 48, 57, 103
coal 58, 89
cobalt 17, 22, 24, 44, 48, 100
Coca-Cola 103
coin 48, 52, 101
coke 58, 61
compact disc (CD) 105
compound 15, 16, 19, 28, 30, 31, 41, 44, 48, 56, 57, 71, 73, 83, 84, 92, 93, 100, 101, 103
salt 30

computer 62, 97
concrete 39, 58, 73
conductivity
  good 14, 23, 44, 48, 53
  poor 14, 76, 80
copernicum 23, 44, 63
copper 23, 25, 41, 44, 48, 54–55, 57, 78, 97, 100, 102
  spider blood 54
  Statue of Liberty 54–55
  uses 41, 57
copper carbonate 54
corrosion 48, 49, 53, 54, 68
crude oil 89
crystal 8, 15, 36, 49, 71, 73, 93
Curie, Marie 65, 66–67, 79, 103
Curie, Pierre 103
curium 23, 25, 44, 63, 67
cyanide 78

D

Dalton, John 102
darmstadtium 22, 25, 44, 63
Davy, Humphry 102
diamond 88, 105
diesel 89
diet 38, 88, 92
distillation 83
DNA 65, 80, 88
drill 48, 72
dubnium 22, 24, 44, 63
Durand, Peter 102
dye 92
dysprosium 23, 25, 44, 62

E

Earth 20, 33, 46–47,

80, 81, 82, 83, 89, 90, 91 94
atmosphere 47, 80, 81, 82, 83, 90, 91, 94
core 46–47
crust 36, 46–47, 83, 92, 94, 97
mantle 46–47
Edison, Thomas 102
Eiffel, Gustave 55
Eiffel Tower 58
Einstein, Albert 63
einsteinium 23, 25, 44, 63, 104
  uses 63
electric motor 16, 62
electricity 33, 48, 53, 54, 63, 68, 89, 101, 102
electron 18, 19, 28, 65
  electron shell 18
Empire State Building 58
erbium 23, 25, 44, 62
europium 22, 25, 44, 62

F

Fabergé, Carl Gustavovich 52
Fahrenheit, Daniel Gabriel 101
fermium 23, 25, 44, 63, 104
fertilizer 80
fire sprinkler system 68
firework 36, 40–41, 48
flame-resistant material 72, 92
fluorescence 94
fluorine 23, 25, 76, 93, 104
  uses 93
fluorite 93
fossil 38, 82

Index

fossil fuel 89, 91
francium 22, 24,
28, 30
half-life 30
radiation 30
fuel 33, 35, 89

G

gadolinium 23,
25, 44, 62
galena 69
gallium 23, 25,
44, 68
uses 68
gamma radiation 65
gas 14, 20, 21, 22, 23,
28, 32, 47, 76–77, 79,
80–83, 90–91
gasoline 17, 89
gemstone 37, 73
germanium 23,
25, 44, 72, 105
uses 72
glass 17, 59, 68, 73,
100
global warming 89
gold 21, 23, 25, 44,
48, 52–53, 97, 100,
101, 102
Aztec and Inca
treasure 53
California gold rush
53, 102
coin 52, 101
conductivity 53
Fabergé egg 53
largest nugget 102
rarity 52, 53
shine 52
space helmet visor
53
uses 52, 53
Golden Gate Bridge 58
Goodyear, Charles
102
GPS 30
graphite 88
greenhouse
effect 91
gunpowder 100
Gutenberg,
Johannes 101

H

Haber, Fritz 103
hafnium 22, 24,
44, 48
half-life 30, 31,
64–65
halogen 16, 23,
76, 92–93
hassium 22, 24,
44, 63
helium 19, 20, 23,
25, 32, 76, 94, 95
uses 95
Hindenburg 34–35,
104
holmium 23, 25,
44, 62
Home Insurance
Building 58
hospital 83
human body 28,
76,78, 80, 82,
84–85, 88
atom 19
bone 38
cell 84, 88
composition of
84–85
digestion 85
enzyme 85
micronutrient 84
nail 85
nerve cell 30, 85
pregnancy 85
tooth 38
hydrocarbon 56, 89
hydrogen 16, 17,
20, 21, 22, 24, 28,
32–33, 35, 56, 84,
88, 95, 101, 103,
104, 105
atomic bomb 63
burning 35
Earth 33, 46
Hindenburg
34–35
power 33
Saturn 32
solar flare 32
Sun 32
water 33
Hydrosol-II 33

I

ibn Hayyān, Jābir
100
Iijima, Sumio 105
indium 23, 25, 44,
68
uses 68
indium tin oxide
68
infrared 53, 72
Internet 54
iodine 23, 25, 65,
76, 84, 92
diet 92
uses 92
iridium 22, 24, 44, 48
iron 16, 21, 22, 24, 44,
45, 46, 48, 50, 54, 56,
57, 58–59, 60–61, 84,
97, 100
blast furnace 60–61
blood 84
construction 58–59
magnetism 59
smelting 58
uses 58–59
weapon 58
Iron Age 58, 100
iron oxide 44–45,
56

J

jet 36, 48
jewelry 48, 53

K

kerosene 89
Kevlar 105
Kilby, Jack 105
krypton 23, 25, 76,
94, 103
uses 94
Kwolek,
Stephanie 105

L

lamp 102
lanthanoid 22–23,
24–25, 44, 62
lanthanum 17,
22, 24, 44, 62
Lascaux caves 56
laser 62, 104
Lavoisier,
Antoine 101
lawrencium 23,
25, 44, 63
lead 23, 25, 44, 56,
57, 65, 68, 69, 78,
97, 100, 101, 105
mine 105
uses 69
Libby, Willard 104
lightbulb 65, 94
limestone 39, 58
Lincoln, Abraham
78
liquid petroleum 89
lithium 20, 22, 24,
30, 97
uses 30, 41
Litvinenko,
Alexander 79
lutetium 23, 25,
44, 62

M

magnesium 16, 22,
24, 28, 36, 45, 46,
84, 104
human brain 84
uses 36, 41
magnetism 16, 44, 59,
62
Magnus, Albertus
100
Maiman, Theodore
104
makeup 72
manganese 17, 22,
24, 44, 48, 84, 100
Mars Exploration
Rover 68
matter 14, 20
states of 14
medical equipment
48, 65
medicine 68, 78
Meganeura 82
meitnerium 22, 24,
44, 63

Mendeleev, Dmitri
22, 102
mendelevium 23,
25, 44, 63
mercury 14, 16, 23,
25, 44, 48, 57, 78,
97, 101
uses 48
metal 11, 14, 22, 28,
44, 48–49, 50–51,
52–53, 58–61, 68–69,
72, 94
metalloid 14, 23,
44, 72–73
allotrope 72
meteorite 20, 22, 47,
58
microchip 53, 97, 105
micronutrient 84
mineral ore 36,
37, 46, 47, 54, 60–61,
68, 69, 72, 97
molecule 19, 33, 71,
82, 83, 84, 85, 88
molybdenum 22,
24, 44, 48
Monet, Claude 79
Moon (Earth's) 46
Mount Everest 47
murder 72, 78–79

N

nanotube 105
naphtha 89
nebula 21
neodymium 16,
22, 24, 44, 62
uses 62
neon 23, 25, 32,
76, 94, 103
uses 94
neptunium 22,
24, 44, 63
neutron 18, 19, 20,
64, 65, 103
nickel 17, 22, 25,
44, 46, 97, 105
uses 48
niobium 22, 24,
44, 48
nitrogen 16, 23,
25, 46, 76, 78, 80,

81, 83, 84, 85, 101,
103, 105
amino acid 85
fertilizer 80
uses 80
nobelium 23, 25,
44, 63
noble gas 23, 76,
94–95, 103
nonmetal 11, 14, 23,
30, 50, 72, 76–77,
80–81, 92–93
nonstick coating 93
nuclear fusion 20,
32
nuclear power 63,
65, 95
nuclear waste 65
nucleus 19, 20, 22,
63, 64
nylon 104, 105

O

oil product 89
oil refinery 37, 49,
88–89
osmium 22, 24,
44, 48
oxygen 8, 15, 16, 17,
19, 23, 25, 32, 36, 38,
44, 45, 46, 54, 58, 61,
71, 73, 76–77, 80, 81,
82–83, 84, 88, 90,
101, 105
blue-green algae
82
burning 82
distillation 83
life 82, 84
photosynthesis 82,
83
uses 83
ozone layer 83

PQ

paint pigment 48,
56–57, 79
palladium 17, 22,
25, 44, 49
uses 49
particle 14, 19

particle accelerator 19, 104
 Large Hadron Collider 19
Pemberton, John 103
pen 48
Pentagon, the 39
periodic table 22–23, 28, 44, 76, 102, 105
Petronas Towers 59
philosopher's stone 100
phosphoric acid 103
phosphorus 23, 25, 38, 76–77, 78, 80, 84, 85, 101, 103
 DNA 80, 85
 fertilizer 80
 human body 80
 uses 80
photosynthesis 82, 83, 90, 91
planet 20
plankton 82
plant 90–91
plastic 16, 17, 89, 104
 PVC 16
platinum 17, 22, 25, 44, 48
Plato 100
plum pudding model (atom) 19
plutonium 22, 24, 44, 63, 64, 65, 104
 uses 63
poison gas 79
pollution 17, 33, 89
polonium 23, 25, 44, 67, 72, 79, 103
poor metal 23, 44, 68–69
potassium 22, 24, 28, 30, 31, 64, 85, 102
 human body 31, 85
potassium nitrate 100
praseodymium 22, 24, 44, 62
precious metal 16
pressure 14
Priestley, Joseph 101

printing 101
promethium 22, 24, 44, 62
protactinium 22, 24, 44, 63
proton 18, 19, 20, 22, 28, 63, 64, 65
pyramid 39

R

radioactive element 30, 31, 63, 64–65, 67, 79, 94, 103
 alpha particle 63, 65
 background radiation 65
 beta particle 65
 decay 31, 64, 92, 94
 gamma ray 65
 strong nuclear force 64
radioactive waste 63
radium 22, 24, 36, 65, 67, 79, 103
 uses 36
radon 23, 25, 65, 76, 94
Ramsey, William 103
rare earth metal 22, 62
rat poison 57, 68
reactive element 15, 23, 25, 28, 30–31, 76
recycling 96–97
reflective element 23
rhenium 22, 24, 44, 48
rhodium 17, 22, 24, 44, 48
rocket 30, 36
roentgenium 23, 25, 44, 63
roofing material 69, 89
rubber 17, 102
rubidium 22, 24, 30
 uses 30
Russell, James T. 105

rust 48, 49, 53, 54, 58, 68
ruthenium 22, 24, 44, 48
Rutherford, Ernest 103
rutherfordium 22, 24, 44, 63

S

samarium 22, 24, 44, 62
satellite 30, 104
 Sputnik I 104
Saturn 32
scandium 22, 24, 44, 62
Scheele, Carl 101
Seaborg, Glenn T. 104
seaborgium 22, 24, 44, 63
selenite 8
selenium 23, 25, 76, 80, 84
 health 80
semiconductor 68, 72, 73, 80
ship 48, 89
silica 71
silicon 17, 23, 25, 44, 46, 71, 72, 73, 97
 uses 73
silicon dioxide 73
silver 23, 25, 44, 48, 69, 97, 100, 105
 mine 105
 uses 48
skyscraper 58–59
smoke detector 63, 65
sodium 15, 22, 24, 28–29, 30, 41, 102, 103
 Dead Sea 30
 sodium chloride (salt) 15, 30
 sodium sulfate 103
 uses 30, 41
solar tower 33
Solomon, King 52
space shuttle 105

Columbia 105
spacecraft 48
star 20–21, 39, 65
 Cassiopeia A 39
 white dwarf 105
stardust 20, 21
steel 11, 16, 17, 50, 55, 58, 59, 72, 83, 102, 105
Stone Age 100
strontium 22, 24, 36
 uses 36, 41
sulfur 8, 17, 23, 25, 36, 46, 56, 76, 80, 100, 102, 103
 bubble gum 103
 uses 80
sulfuric acid 80
Sun 32, 33 53, 83, 90, 91
 ultraviolet (UV) ray 83
supernova 20, 21, 39, 64
synthetic element 14
synthetic product 104, 105

T

Taipei 101 59
tantalum 22, 24, 44, 48
technetium 22, 24, 44, 48
Teflon 104
telephone 54, 102
television 30, 97
tellurium 23, 25, 44, 64, 72
temperature 14, 33, 45, 61, 76
terbium 23, 25, 44, 62
thallium 23, 25, 44, 68
 uses 68
thermometer 48, 101
Thomson, J. J. 19
thorium 22, 24, 44, 63
thulium 23, 25, 44, 62

tin 11, 23, 25, 44, 68, 97, 100, 101
 tin can 102
 uses 68
tin oxide 68
Titan 80
titanium 22, 24, 41, 44, 48, 97, 104, 105
 uses 41, 48
titanium oxide 56
TNT 81
tool 37, 58
tooth 38, 48
toothpaste 36, 93
touch screen 68
toxic element 36, 56, 57, 69, 72, 78–79, 100, 102
track cycling 86–87
transition metal 22, 23, 41, 44, 48–49, 50, 56, 68
tungsten 22, 24, 44, 48, 69
 uses 48, 94
tungsten carbide 48
Tutankhamen 52

U

Universe 19, 20–21, 32
 Big Bang 20
unnamed element 23, 25, 105
unreactive element 76, 80–81, 94–95
ununhexium 23, 25, 44, 63
ununquadium 23, 25, 44, 63
uraninite 36
uranite 30
uranium 21, 22, 24, 44, 63, 64, 65, 69, 94, 104
 uses 63, 104

V

van Beethoven, Ludwig 78
van Gogh, Vincent 56–57, 79, 103

vanadium 16, 22, 24, 44, 48, 105
Volta, Alessandro 101, 102

W

water 28–29, 30, 33, 46, 49, 69, 82, 84
weapon 54, 58, 65, 100
welding 94
White, Edward 53
wind turbine 62
Wright, Orville and Wilbur 103

X

xenon 16, 23, 25, 76, 94
 uses 94

Y

Ytterby 62
ytterbium 23, 25, 44, 62
yttrium 22, 24, 44, 62
 uses 62

Z

zinc 23, 25, 44, 48, 84, 101
zinc oxide 56
zirconium 22, 24, 44, 48
 uses 41

Credits and acknowledgments